THE ENCHANTED HILL

THE STORY OF HEARST CASTLE AT SAN SIMEON

THE ENCHANTED HILL

THE STORY OF HEARST CASTLE AT SAN SIMEON

BY
CARLETON M. WINSLOW, JR.
AND
NICKOLA L. FRYE

WITH A SPECIAL SUPPLEMENT BY
TAYLOR COFFMAN
SENIOR GUIDE, HEARST CASTLE

CELESTIAL ARTS
MILLBRAE, CALIFORNIA

Produced for Celestial Arts by

Rosebud Books, Inc.
8777 Lookout Mountain Avenue
Los Angeles, CA 90046

Jacket and book design by Laura LiPuma

Library of Congress Cataloging in Publication Data

Winslow, Carleton, 1919-
The enchanted hill.
1. Hearst-San Simeon State Historical Monument.
2. Hearst, William Randolph, 1863-1951.   I. Title.
F868.S18W53   979.4'78   79-56890

ISBN 0-89087-198-1

The book is dedicated, of course, to the members
of the Hearst Family and their many guests and friends
who were enchanted by the Hill, and, over the years,
leant enchantment to it.

Acknowledgements

This book reflects, without reflecting upon, the following people who have
generously given of time and knowledge: John Beach, Berkeley, CA; Sara Holmes
Boutelle, Santa Cruz, CA; Mary Cooper, San Luis Obispo, CA; Louisiana Clayton
Dart, San Luis Obispo, CA; Winton Frey, San Luis Obispo, CA; Charles Gates,
San Luis Obispo, CA; Kenneth Haggard, San Luis Obispo, CA;
Irene Horne, Morro Bay, CA; Daniel Kreigir, San Luis Obispo, CA;
and Ken Murray, Beverly Hills, CA.

The many remarkable photographs which illustrate the book have been
generously provided by Ken Raveill, Baron Wolman, John White, Jeff Hosier
and Jim Englund, Mrs. Mable Souza, Marjorie Ramsey, Diana Peterson, The
Bancroft Library of The University of California, Berkeley and the Architecture
Department at California Polytechnic State University, San Luis Obispo.

A special thanks to Gerald Fiahlo, Director of the Castle for making
available his time and energy, and to his colleague, Ann Miller, for her invaluable
assistance in locating photographs and documents. And to Ron Whaley of Ogden
Food Service, San Simeon California for his generously given counsel and advice
throughout.

To Reginald and Helen Hennessey of Los Angeles for encouraging us at the
outset, and to Laura LiPuma, Don Ackland and the staff of Rosebud Books
for making it all a reality.

In addition, Taylor Coffman of the Hearst Castle staff read the manuscript
and made many invaluable suggestions. And, in last place alphabetically but in
first place in love and knowledge of the Castle is Mr. Woodrow Yost who, over a
period of ten years, has been contributing to this book.

Lastly, we would like to acknowledge our families, Charlotte, Constance
and Jan Winslow of San Luis Obispo, CA, and Phillip, Tracy, and Jennifer Frye
of Petaluma, CA. Without their love and understanding the research and
writing of this book would have been impossible.

PREFACE

This book is designed to enhance and enrich your visit to Hearst Castle, to prepare you in advance for the trip, or to reinforce the sights and sounds of your memory. It can also be used as a guide for people who cannot experience the Enchanted Hill first hand. It is the authors' hope that this work, including the annotated bibliography, will lead others to explore in greater depth the multi-dimensional aspects of the Enchanted Hill. Because the State of California decided to maintain the estate as William Randolph Hearst left it when he departed San Simeon for the last time, the buildings are free of the dry environment associated with many museums. Yet as a consequence of this many of the artifacts are not well lighted, nor are they displayed close enough to the visitor. The Castle can be seen only as part of scheduled tours. The Administration and Guide departments at the monument constantly review the content of the tours; however, the increasing attendance — close to a million visitors in 1979 — makes tours of greater duration or depth impossible.

It is hoped that *The Enchanted Hill* will assist the visitor, the specialist, or the general reader with the necessary historical details and provide an artistic catalogue, certainly not complete, to set the stage for one's visit or armchair appreciation of the Castle, its setting, or the Collection.

A word should be added here about source material. In the absence of books and articles, the authors have relied heavily on correspondence and interviews, most of which are duly recorded in the bibliography. Rumor and lore about the Castle abound and the authors have tried to check all information. Some material was given to the authors with the understanding that the source would not be revealed. Material of questionable veracity has not been used. This is a work of appreciation — of the man, of his Castle, and of his art collection. *The Enchanted Hill* represents a personal statement, something certainly with which not everyone is expected to agree. For the specialist, as you will see, there is much to criticize about the many structures or the Collection. But for both the specialist and the visitor there is much wonderment, enchantment, and pleasure about the Castle, its setting, or the Collection.

In general the authors agree on the interpretation of the information. However, both authors have felt free to inject judgments of their own into the work. In general when the first person is used, Mr. Winslow is making a judgment of his own. Each reader of this book is free to communicate with the authors or the publisher. We would especially appreciate additional information to supplement our existing knowledge.

C H A P T E R   1

THE ENCHANTED HILL: AN INTRODUCTION

Over half a century ago a man named William Randolph Hearst began to fulfill a dream. He had inherited property from his mother and father which included fifty miles of shoreline on a remote stretch of the Pacific Coast, halfway between San Francisco and Los Angeles, and encompassed over two hundred and fifty thousand acres of land. The total area was approximately one-half the size of the state of Rhode Island. The future site of the Castle was sixteen hundred feet above the sea, and on a clear day Mr. Hearst could look West across the sparkling Pacific Ocean toward the Orient. But it was more satisfying to look north and east for the most distant blue mountains belonged to him. He called the spot La Cuesta Encantada — The Enchanted Hill.

Today William Randolph Hearst, his wife Millicent, his close friend Marion Davies, his architect Julia Morgan, and the host of friends, acquaintances, and associates who haunted the Castle have vanished from the Enchanted Hill, but the structures which they built and enjoyed remain enlivened by nearly a million visitors each year. The visitors are drawn to the Castle by the view, the gardens, the buildings, and the collection, but most of all they are drawn by the mystique that permeates the name of Hearst Castle.

Visitors to the Castle are full of questions. What style is it? How many books are there in the library? How much did it cost to build? How many people worked there in its heyday? Why was it left unfinished? The key question to be asked is,

At once imposing and picturesque, 100-room La Casa Grande reaches skyward from the Main Terrace.

The gardens abound in snow-white marble statuary. Here, a copy of the "Venus of Cyrene."

What *is* Hearst Castle? Each person will conclude his or her own answer, but we would like to offer some suggestions culled from years of observation and bountiful suggestions.

Hearst Castle is a group of buildings which function as a villa or country house, in the shape of an Italian hill town, which we know is usually dominated by a cathedral or monastery. In no sense of the word is Mr. Hearst's edifice a "castle". That word implies defense, and although it did protect the owner from the curious, it lacks the architectural features generally associated with castles.

Some have regarded it as a rich man's plaything, the largest toy in the world. And, indeed, Mr. Hearst appears to have taken an almost childlike delight in the enterprise. He was anxious for others to enjoy his plaything as well. In a letter to his architect, Julia Morgan, on October 18, 1927, he says:

Miss Julia Morgan
Merchant Exchange Building
San Francisco, California

Dear Miss Morgan:
I am leaving for the East tomorrow, Wednesday night. I have a few last words, as it were, to say about the Hill.

I think we must positively proceed immediately to build certain animal houses and shelters. I thought at one time that it was desirable to hide the houses in places where they would not be particularly conspicuous, but I find that the animals collect around such feeding places and shelters in distant spots, and we would have our animals where we would never see them.

I would suggest, therefore, that we make these shelters exceedingly picturesque log houses and put them in certain picturesque locations not far from the main road. There are a number of tree clumps along the road where such shelters could be picturesquely located.

Will you kindly have these locations picked out at your earliest convenience?

I think the giraffes should be transferred from where they are. Nobody yet who has come to the ranch has seen the giraffes.

If you want to consult me about the locations, I suggest that you make the locations and then send me a road map with the locations marked on it, and perhaps some photographs and sketches of what it is proposed to do . . .

Sincerely,
W.R. Hearst

The Roman god Neptune stands in the pediment of an ancient Italian temple; the swimming pool below is named after him.

La Casa Grande's lower facade section is reminiscent of a Northern Spanish cathedral. The dark wood gable on the third floor lends an exotic, Oriental flavor to the building.

Perfect symmetry; the tranquil Indoor Swimming Pool.

Clearly, his purpose in collecting paintings, sculptures, and giraffes was to delight his friends.

In addition to the *Expanded Toy Box Theory* to explain Mr. Hearst's motivation, we list the following:

The Expanded Camp Theory. The Hill and its buildings can be considered a camp made permanent. La Casa Grande is the great communal tent and the guest houses are the sleeping tents clustered around. This idea is reinforced by the fact that the hill was originally a campsite and that the use of catsup, A-1 sauce and mustard jars, which so delight the visitor, seems consistent with that idea.

The Warehouse Museum Theory. That the buildings were designed to contain one of the largest personal art collections in the world can hardly be disputed. The size and shape of many rooms were dictated more by the characteristics of the contents, such as the tapestries, than by the habitability of the rooms.

The Corporate Headquarters Theory. The Enchanted Hill certainly was a corporate headquarters for all of the Hearst corporations and subsidiaries in the sense that it was contained in the person of Mr. Hearst himself, just as Charlemagne, the early King of the Franks, had no fixed capitol and moved most of the Court of the Holy Roman Empire with him. However, except for the Gothic Study and the offices to the east of it, there are few hallmarks of international corporate business.

There are no files and no business machines — just a boardroom and a multiplicity of telephones.

The Resort Hotel Theory. The Enchanted Hill is sometimes perceived as a motel in lavish scale, a sort of celestial Boca Raton where everything is free, except the telephone bill. The hilltop functioned for the pleasure of Mr. Hearst, a theory to be further explored in Chapter IV, "Heaven on a Hilltop." For an expanded account of this phase of Castle life we refer you to *The Golden Days of San Simeon* by Ken Murray and to several other books listed in the bibliography.

The Phoebe Apperson Hearst Memorial Building Theory. Mr. Hearst's mother died just before the planning and construction of the Castle had begun. As an only child, Mr. Hearst had been much closer to his mother than to his father or to anybody else in the family. While he did not always conduct his private affairs as his mother would have wished, and she did not hesitate in letting him know her disapproval, he still had the highest regard for her.

Plants and works of art, including the huge wellhead on the South Terrace, were brought to the Castle from his mother's home in Pleasanton. The continual recurrence of the Madonna theme throughout the Castle has suggested to some people that the whole enterprise was at least in part a memorial to his mother, of whom he was so inordinately fond.

With such widely differing definitions of the nature and

function of the Castle, it is understandable that this group of buildings should appeal to people of many interests beyond art and architecture. There are elements of uniqueness in its construction engineering; ornamental horticulture; furniture design; motion picture personalities; restoration and rehabilitation; social history of the 1920s and 1930s; journalism; Indian and early Spanish colonial history; wrought iron; ceramics; Spanish history; oriental rugs; Persian tile and pottery; Greek pottery; silver; San Luis Obispo County history; botany; Greek and Roman history and mythology; tapestries; and zoology.

Clearly, no one need feel left out because he or she is not an art historian. So diversified are the areas of interest touched on by the Enchanted Hill that no one book, short of an encyclopedia, can address them all.

The rich history that lies behind the land, the people, the gardens, the architecture, and the collection contains some measure of controversy and mystery, and if these two qualities are used as crude standards, surely Hearst Castle must rank as one of the most intriguing buildings in Western civilization.

A harmony of light, space, and form makes the Neptune Pool the architectural gem of the Enchanted Hill.

Below the Castle the grassy hills of the Hearst Ranch slope gently to the coastal plain. Cattle have grazed this land since the early mission days.

C H A P T E R 2

GEORGE HEARST
AND PHOEBE APPERSON HEARST

The central coast of California upon which William Randolph Hearst built his ranch has a long and varied history. It was first hunted in prehistoric times by the Salinan Indians, who occupied these rugged areas of the south-central coast. The boundaries of their territory have been obliterated by time, but the area can be defined as stretching from the sea to the main ridge of the Coast Range and from southern Monterey County (Soledad) to parts of northern San Luis Obispo County. The interior is dominated by heavily wooded hills and the mountains of the southern Coast Range. The sea coast consists of sheer cliffs and rocky beaches.

The Salinans, who lived in villages, were a hunting and gathering people. They moved seasonally when necessary to obtain food or other supplies. They traded with their eastern neighbors, the Yokuts, and somewhat with their southern neighbors, the Chumash.

In 1769, Juan Gaspar de Portolá led a Spanish expedition through the Salinan territory. Two years later, in July 1771, Mission San Antonio de Padua, founded by the Franciscan order, became the first mission to be established in this area. Mission San Miguel Archangel was founded in July of 1797, in the southern Salinan area. The records of the two missions show that over 3,000 Indians became neophytes. The Indians were taught agriculture, stock raising and weaving skills.

The mission experience caused a tremendous decline in the Salinan population. By 1831 there were fewer than 700 and by

The abrupt projection of San Simeon Point provides one of the the very few safe anchorages along a rugged stretch of California coastline.

1928 the California Mission rolls showed there were only 36 Salinans left.

Rancho San Simeon, which belonged to the missions, was secularized in 1836, and divided into three great ranchos: San Simeon, which consisted of 4,468 acres; Santa Rosa with 13,183 acres; and Piedra Blanca, the largest with 49,000 acres.

By 1852, a whaling station had been established at San Simeon Point on the land adjacent to the natural bay of San Simeon. The whalers practiced shore whaling. Small boats went out and intercepted the migrating whales. The dead whales were towed to shore and cut up and hoisted onto the wharf, where the oil was rendered in huge trypots. Artifacts connected with whaling are on display at Sebastion's Store in the village of San Simeon.

A village grew up around the whaling activities which included a general store, a blacksmith shop, a barbershop, and a saloon. Twenty-two families lived in San Simeon and were employed by the whaling station and on the ranchos. In 1865, George Hearst purchased 45,000 acres, including all of the San Simeon Ranch.

George Hearst, the father of William Randolph Hearst, was born in Missouri in 1820, the son of William and Elizabeth Hearst. Because of the isolation of the farm and the need for his labor, George Hearst found it difficult as a child to attend school. He learned to read and write, but his practical educa-

tion involved learning about the earth from neighboring miners, and geology and mineralogy from books borrowed from Dr. Silas Reed, a neighbor.

In the spring of 1850, George Hearst followed the lure of gold to California. He was better equipped to succeed at wrenching a living from the earth than many others seeking gold. He crossed the continent by horse and was fully prepared to face the hardships of making his fortune by mining.

After ten lean years in the mines in California, Hearst and two partners, Melville Atwood and A.E. Head, struck it rich. Near Virginia City, Nevada, they had purchased a half interest in a claim. Their mine, which proved to contain no gold, was part of the Comstock Lode and assayed rich in silver. With the profits, George Hearst was able to purchase a one-sixth interest in another Comstock mine, the Ophir, which profited at $2,200 a ton.

In 1860, George Hearst, learning that his mother was ill, returned to Missouri. After her death, his thoughts turned to Phoebe Apperson, the daughter of a Missouri neighbor.

Phoebe Elizabeth Apperson was born in Missouri into an old Virginia family on December 3, 1842. Her parents, Randolph and Drusilla, were prosperous slave owners with a large farm on the Meramec River. They occupied a social position of some standing in their community. Phoebe was a tiny woman with Dresden doll features. She spoke precise English and had

An early photograph of Phoebe Apperson Hearst.

One of the great empire-builders of nineteenth century America, George Hearst.

Verification of the Rancho San Simeon land grant (on file in the Bancroft Library, Berkeley).

learned French, an unusual achievement in rural Missouri.

But the courtship of George Hearst and Phoebe was complicated. He was forty years old and uncouth in both appearance and manner. He drank, chewed tobacco and swore. He was hardly the epitome of a proper suitor for eighteen-year-old Phoebe.

To Phoebe, George Hearst represented exotic lands, adventure and romance. In the bargain he was a handsome man. Her parents objected to the union and caused a year's delay in the matrimonial plans.

Miss Apperson took the situation into her own hands when she and George Hearst eloped. They were married in Stedman, Missouri on June 15, 1862. The newlyweds took the luxury route to California in October of the same year. They traveled by train to New York, by boat to Panama, across the isthmus, and then boarded another vessel to San Francisco. The pregnant Phoebe was in great discomfort on the Pacific leg of their journey. On board ship were Mr. and Mrs. David Peck and their two-year-old son Orrin, who would later paint the portrait of William Randolph Hearst which hangs in the Gothic Study. The families remained friends all their lives.

As they sailed through the Golden Gate, the untraveled Phoebe grew excited by the raw and bustling city. "I intend to live on these hills where I can always see the bay," she proclaimed. And in Stevenson House atop a San Francisco hill, on

The original ranch house of 1878, built by Senator Hearst and still in use today.

Phoebe Apperson Hearst and two of her grandchildren.

a cold April night in 1863, Phoebe Apperson Hearst gave birth to her only child, William Randolph Hearst.

In 1865, George Hearst purchased the Piedra Blanca Rancho for thirty thousand dollars. He improved the port of San Simeon, and built a new wharf in 1878. He later bought the Santa Rosa Rancho, and used all three parcels of land for raising horses and dairy cattle.

In January of 1887, George Hearst was elected to the United States Senate by the California Legislature. Senator Hearst died from "a serious derangement of the bowels," according to the New York Times, on March 1, 1891, in Washington D.C. He left every penny of his $18,000,000 estate to his widow, Phoebe, who was at the time 48 years old. Later William Randolph was to write to his mother:

> My father never did a better thing than when he made the will he did. I have admired him for it and have been happy to concur in it, and I have never told you how many times I have been advised by fools and scoundrels otherwise. That is the kind of thing for our own kind of people, and I hope to so live that you will have as much confidence in me as my father had in you. I hope too that I will never live to read your will, and that you will live as long as I do and that we both shall be as happy as I am now.
> Affectionately and gratefully,
> "Will"

On April 13, 1919, at the age of seventy-six, Phoebe Hearst died. She left the bulk of her $11,000,000 estate, including the land at San Simeon, to her son. Her parting marked a significant change in William Randolph Hearst's life.

Mr. Hearst was then fifty-five years old, an age when some men think of choosing comfortable shoes and easy chairs. William Randolph Hearst, too, retired in a sense. It was clear that despite drive, effort, and money, success in politics eluded him. World War I was drawing to a close. Perhaps all these events accidently coincided, but the fact remains that during the fall of 1919, W. R. Hearst found himself making his way to the Merchant's Exchange Building in San Francisco for an encounter with a woman named Julia Morgan, an architect. This occasion would prove to be the first step toward beginning work on the buildings at San Simeon. Between the two World Wars much of the enthusiasm, drive, effort, and love which he had previously given to politics, travel, and his mother were now poured into a new dream.

Mission San Antonio in the 1870s, located on the northeast perimeter of the original 250,000-acre Hearst property.

The Mission warehouse today.

Spanish Colonial-style house in San Simeon Village. Built about 1930, it serves today as the private residence of a retired Hearst Ranch foreman.

A masterpiece of romantic design, La Casa Grande soars cathedral-like from its hilltop setting.

C H A P T E R 3

THE MAN, HIS ARCHITECT AND HIS CASTLE

"... Miss Morgan, we are tired of camping out in the open
at the ranch in San Simeon and I would like to build a little
something ..."

The Man

The fragment of conversation displayed above is part of a discussion which took place on the thirteenth floor of the Merchant's Exchange Building in San Francisco in 1919. The speaker, William Randolph Hearst, was talking to Julia Morgan, the family architect. Both were about to embark on a building project which spanned a quarter of a century.

William Randolph Hearst had spent fifty-six tumultuous years before this auspicious encounter. As a child, "Willie" attended both a private school and Lincoln Grammar School. As preparation for the world, it was his father's decision to send him to a rough-and-tumble public school.

When he was ten his mother took him on an extended year-and-a-half tour of Europe. Taking a keen interest in all he saw, he was no ordinary child tourist. He delighted in the strange languages, exotic foods, and differing customs to which his mother fondly exposed his maturing intellect. With her guidance, he toured art galleries, museums and historic monuments. During this first trip to Europe he embarked on his lifelong passion for collecting. These early collections, which were as zealously pursued, concentrated on stamps, coins, beer steins, porcelain and German comic books.

Mr. Hearst attended four additional San Francisco primary schools and at the age of sixteen returned to Europe with his mother and his tutor, Thomas Barry, for several months of touring and collecting. While Phoebe remained behind to benefit from the curative waters of Germany, Barry escorted

The sum of its parts; the Neptune Pool, the three cottages, and La Casa Grande on the Enchanted Hill.

William to Concord, New Hampshire to be enrolled in Saint Paul's School. With this first experience of separation from his mother, and the isolation at boarding school, "Willie" turned lonely and homesick. He appears to have dropped out in 1881 and to have returned home to be privately tutored before entering Harvard. Hearst, at this time, was a tall, slender, shy youth, with a high, soft voice that never deepened or changed.

In the fall of 1882, he went to Harvard University accompanied by his mother who procured and furnished a suitable room for him. Most academic subjects bored him and he enrolled in and dropped Latin, Greek, and Philosophy during his first year. He continued with German since he was familiar with it. Harvard took itself seriously and was not prepared for William Randolph Hearst.

"I am beginning to get awfully tired of this place," he wrote his mother after only a few weeks, "and I long to get out west somewhere where I can stretch myself without coming in contact with the narrow walls with which the prejudice of the bean eaters has surrounded us. I long to get out in the woods and breathe the fresh mountain air and listen to the moaning of the pines. It makes me almost crazy with homesickness when I think of it. I hate this weak, pretty New England scenery with its gentle rolling hills, its pea green foliage, its vistas, tame enough to begin with but totally disfigured by houses

and barns which could not be told apart save for the respective inhabitants, I hate it as I do a weak pretty face without force of character. I long to see our own woods, the jagged rocks and towering mountains, the majestic pines, the grand impressive scenery of the far West. I shall never live anywhere but in California. I like to be away for awhile only to appreciate it the more when I return."

He had friends and followers at Harvard, those who cluster around a generous spender, and those who follow a colorful leader. Through his association with the "Harvard Lampoon", he did, however, develop a taste for the news media. Here he met the philosopher George Santayana. He developed an early enthusiasm for the theater and attended productions in Boston whenever possible. A persistent enjoyment of practical jokes eventually reached such proportions, as for example in celebrating the victory of Grover Cleveland over James G. Blaine, that Harvard suspended him short of his junior year.*

His mother joined him in Washington D.C. to serve out his suspension from Harvard. To his unbridled enthusiasm for practical jokes, journalism, and collecting, he now added a taste for politics which he pursued with vigor for the next

*There appear to be several versions of Mr. Hearst's expulsion from Harvard. Compare this version with W. A. Swanberg's in *Citizen Hearst,* page 39 of the paperback edition.

Millicent Willson Hearst with twin sons, Randolph and David.

William Randolph Hearst as a Harvard undergraduate (early 1880s).

Phoebe Apperson Hearst's estate located in Pleasanton. The "Hacienda" was frequently visited by Mr. Hearst and his family.

One of Mr. Hearst's sons at the "Hacienda." The Renaissance well-head is now located on the South Terrace at the Enchanted Hill.

twenty-four years. While in Washington, William Randolph attended sessions of Congress, visited national monuments, and immersed himself in United States history. The study of history was pursued with a determination equal to his other hobbies. His collections had expanded into other areas, most particularly books, which included a $2,000 rare edition of Alexander Hamilton's *Federalist Papers*.

The year 1886 was epochal for W. R. Hearst, as he called himself at that time. His father was appointed United States Senator to fill the unexpired term of Senator John T. Miller, who died in mid-March, 1886. At the same time, William was gaining new insights into the potential power of the press by working for Joseph Pulitzer's newspaper, *The New York World*. The paper's journalistic advocacy for France's gift to the people of the United States, the Statue of Liberty, resulted in its raising $100,000 in 1885 to build the supporting pedestal. By 1887, Hearst was applying all he had learned from Pulitzer to *The San Francisco Examiner,* which had been given to him by his father.

W. A. Swanberg, one of Mr. Hearst's biographers, writes that William so devoted himself to the *Examiner* that he wrote to his mother saying, "I don't suppose that I shall live more than three or four years if this strain keeps up. I don't get to bed until two o'clock and I wake up about seven in the morning and can't get to sleep again, for I must see the paper and compare it with the *Chronicle*. If we are best, I can turn over and go to sleep with quiet satisfaction, but if the *Chronicle* happens to scoop us, that lets me out of all sleep for the day ... Thank Heaven for one thing, our efforts are appreciated. The great and good people of California want the *Examiner*."

In 1891, Senator George Hearst died in Washington, leaving his entire fortune to his wife, Phoebe. At the time of his death his son had already revived the moribund *San Francisco Examiner*. Through a combination of publicity and innovative journalistic techniques, he made himself and his paper famous. Looking for new worlds to conquer, he gained a foothold in the New York publishing field. He purchased the New York *Morning Journal* in preference to *The Times, The Recorder*, and *The Advertiser*, which had higher price tags. Although the *Journal* was at that time a weak newspaper, Hearst thereby established himself in New York. Phoebe, with some reluctance, financed the venture by selling her seven-sixteenth interest in the Anaconda Copper Mining Company for $7,500,000. The *Morning Journal* became the flagship of the Hearst Fleet. The expansion of his publishing empire into New York was only part of a larger master plan. His ultimate goal was the Presidency of the United States. Hearst walked straight into the center of New York City politics and in 1908 was elected to the House of Representatives, his only real political success. It has been suggested that building the Castle at San Simeon grew out of his political frustrations. Whether or not this is true can be argued; however, it must be remembered that he began plans to build at San Simeon in 1919. Mr. Hearst remained both a force and a threat in New York City and State politics well into the year 1924, at which time he was sixty-one.

In 1924, Alfred E. Smith won the Governorship of New York by 257,000 votes, defeating the Hearst-backed Republican, Ogden Mills.

As if to compensate for the loss, Hearst purchased, in 1926, a tenth-century Spanish cloister from the Province of Segovia for $120,000. The Segovia Cloister, costing an additional $360,000 to move, remained in storage in Mr. Hearst's famous five-story Bronx warehouse and was part of the 1941 forced liquidation. The Segovia Cloister is not to be confused with the Cistercian monastery Santa Maria de Oliva, which would have been erected in Golden Gate Park had it not caught fire and burned.

Mr. Hearst's political failures did not diminish his thirst for real estate acquisition and building. The construction of the Hacienda at Jolon (1930); the new work at Wyntoon in Shasta County on the McCloud River (1930); the Florenz Ziegfield, the largest theater in the United States (1925); the Warrick Hotel in New York (1925); and the Santa Monica Beach House (110 rooms and fifty-five bathrooms), cost an estimated $1,000,000. After the purchase of the medieval castle of St. Donat's, a fortune was poured into improvements, such as the addition

A pen and ink drawing of William Randolph Hearst as a young man.

A warmly smiling William Randolph Hearst in a photograph taken in the 1930s.

The original Wyntoon designed by Bernard Maybeck for Phoebe Apperson Hearst. The structure was destroyed by fire in 1930.

of a swimming pool, three tennis courts, and a banquet hall. Mr. Hearst went on to purchase whole sections of Hamilton Palace in Scotland, which was sagging because of underground coal mining tunnels. His holdings in Mexico included a thousand square miles of land in Vera Cruz, Campeche, and Yucatan and a million acre ranch known as Babicora in Chihuahua. For a while he also owned the Ritz Towers in New York valued at $6,000,000, which was handed over to the mortgage holder in the late 1930s because funds were not available to keep up the payments. He also purchased the enormous estate of Mrs. O.H.P. Belmont in Long Island for his wife, Millicent Hearst, complete with drawbridge and moat. (He married the former Millicent Willson on April 28, 1903.) In addition, he owned the elaborate quarters at the Clarendon Hotel in New York, which became his official "home," and an entire floor of rooms in the Ambassador Hotel in Los Angeles. He later built a fourteen-room bungalow on the Metro-Goldwyn-Mayer lot for Marion Davies.

These purchases and building projects consumed much time and attention, but San Simeon was always his favorite project. It flourished under the joint guidance of Mr. Hearst and Julia Morgan, and became the physical embodiment of the man's dream.

An early student drawing by Julia Morgan dated ''Venice, August 1899.''

Possibly the first sketch for the Enchanted Hill by Miss Morgan. The note in Miss Morgan's hand refers to the "Ronda" motif of the single tower and facade of La Casa Grande.

Another accomplished student work, a wash drawing by Julia Morgan.

His Architect: Julia Morgan

Julia Morgan had come to the attention of the Hearst family when she was working on the Hearst Mining Building at the University of California at Berkeley. Phoebe Apperson Hearst would naturally have been interested in her since at the time she was employed by John Galen Howard, architect for the Berkeley campus of the University of California. Mrs. Hearst had met Miss Morgan in Paris a number of years previously.

Julia Morgan was born in San Francisco on January 26, 1872. Her father, Charles "Bill" Morgan, was a small dapper man, who dabbled in a multiplicity of not too successful businesses. Her mother, Eliza Parmalee Morgan, was the daughter of a millionaire speculator. Julia had three brothers and a younger sister.

The Morgan family lived in a fashionable suburb of Oakland, in a Victorian style house built in the 1870s. As a child Julia was small and frail. She was closeted when young because of poor health, but she soon rebelled and became a tomboy. She was stubborn and fearless, two qualities which would serve her well throughout life. At school she was an excellent student and applied her energies to obtain a fine education.

In the fall of 1890, at the age of eighteen, Julia enrolled in the University of California at Berkeley, one of about two dozen coeds in a previously all male school. In her sophomore year Miss Morgan decided to become an architect. Her mother's cousin, Pierre Le Brun, a New York City architect, might have been an inspiration. The university had no architecture curriculum at the time. Starting in the College of Engineering, she obtained her degree in civil engineering. One of her instructors, Bernard Maybeck, also taught private classes in architecture at his home in Berkeley and Julia attended. Her engineering background is evident in much of her work. In fact,

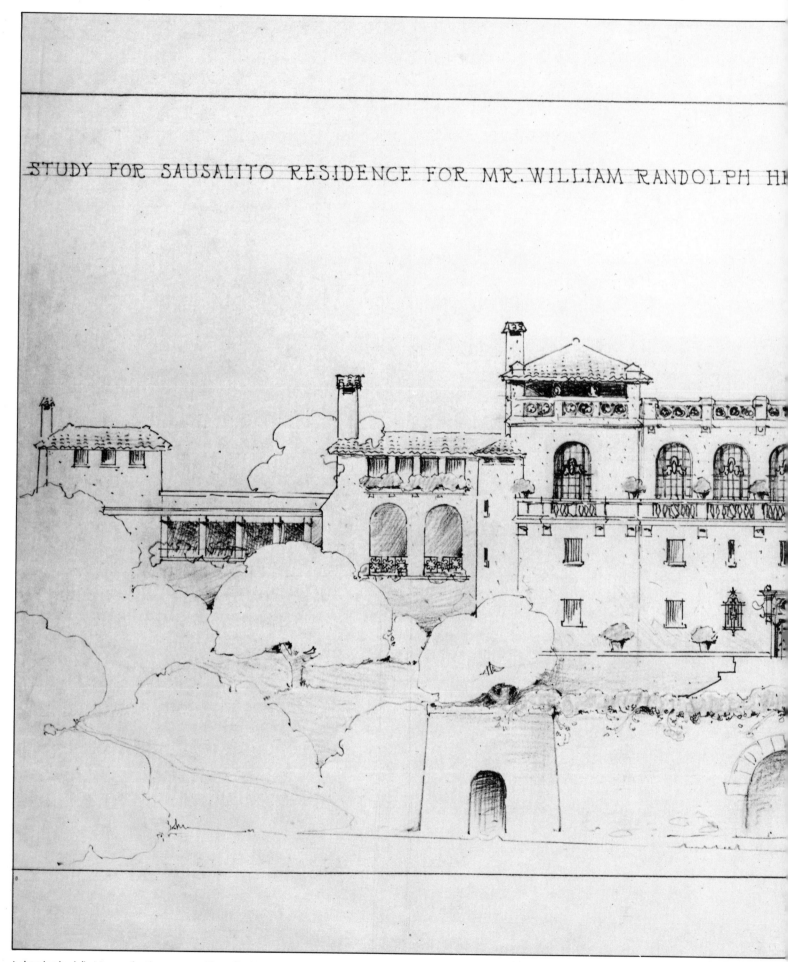

STUDY FOR SAUSALITO RESIDENCE FOR MR. WILLIAM RANDOLPH HE

A drawing by Julia Morgan for the proposed Sausalito House. The project was abandoned when Phoebe Hearst died and Mr. Hearst inherited the San Simeon property.

Simplified Scheme . as J. M et M. O.P. decided.
given up!

A further study of La Casa Grande which attempts to reconcile the "cathedral/house" design.

one of the outstanding characteristics of her buildings is the deft, logical, and beautiful way she integrates structure and architecture.

After graduation in 1894, Maybeck encouraged her to go to Paris to study at the L'École des Beaux-Arts, the most prestigious architectural school of the time. What he failed to mention was that the Beaux-Arts did not, in fact, admit female students, and particularly foreign female students. In 1898, after much persistence on her part and with the help of Maybeck and others, she was finally admitted as the institution's first female student.

She was evidently the first woman to graduate from the school and, in fact, was required to do some of the work a second time. She was certainly skillful in what she did. In addition to regular school work, she took trips around France sketching facades, buildings, and fountains.

She completed her course of study, which was very traditional in nature, in three years. She studied planning logic, ornamentation, and classic detailing. She drew from these resources in her later odyssey of design with William Randolph Hearst.

Julia returned to the United States in late 1901 or early 1902, at the age of thirty, with a degree in architecture. Shortly thereafter she won a job working with John Galen Howard. Mr. Howard was directing the designing of several of the

Julia Morgan, the architect for the Hearst family.

This drawing establishes the twin-tower concept which now shows bells and considerable embellishment.

The tower of this early seventeenth century Spanish Renaissance church, Santa Maria la Major in Ronda, Spain, bears a striking resemblance to Julia Morgan's first sketch of the Hearst Castle facade.

buildings financed by Phoebe Hearst for the university campus at Berkeley. Julia also worked with Bernard Maybeck on a large vacation home, Wyntoon, to be located on the McCloud River.

In addition, Phoebe Hearst asked Miss Morgan to remodel the Hacienda in Pleasanton. It was here in 1902 that Miss Morgan met William Randolph Hearst. Julia found her client's son knowledgeable about architecture. With the support of the Hearst family and friends, she opened her own office soon after completing her education and apprenticeship. However, it would be an error to charge her success exclusively to the Hearsts. She was a hard worker, a highly competent, if not brilliant, designer. During her life she was responsible for possibly over 800 buildings, which is a huge body of work for an individual practitioner. (In her will Julia Morgan requested that her drawings and her office records be destroyed. The exact number and the location of many of her buildings may never be known.) At the time she was engaged to design the buildings at the ranch in San Simeon, she was already a leading designer of custom homes in the San Francisco Bay area. She had completed numerous larger non-commercial structures at Asilomar in Pacific Grove, and St. John's Presbyterian Church in Berkeley. She had not, however, done anything the size of Hearst Castle, but that hardly mattered since all that Mr. Hearst asked for was "... a little something."

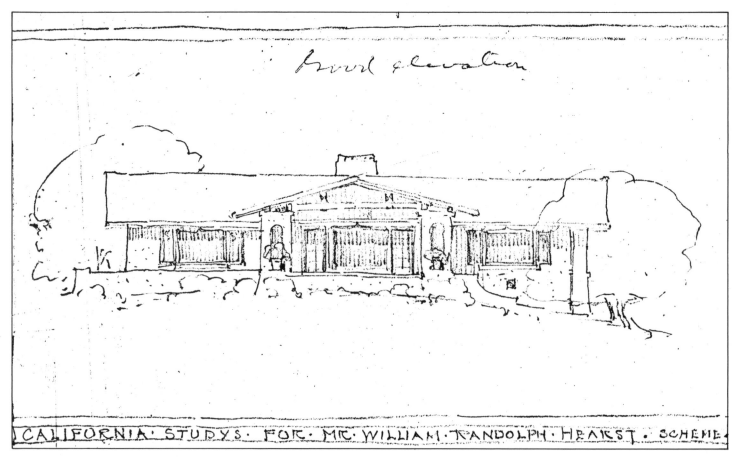

Scheme M, a study for one of the bungalows on the hill.

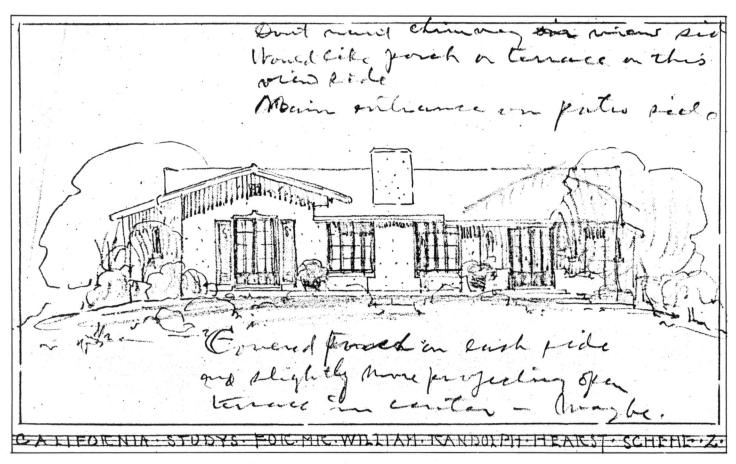

Scheme 2 with Mr. Hearst's handwritten note to put the chimney on the other side, so that a porch or terrace might be designed
for the main entrance or patio side.

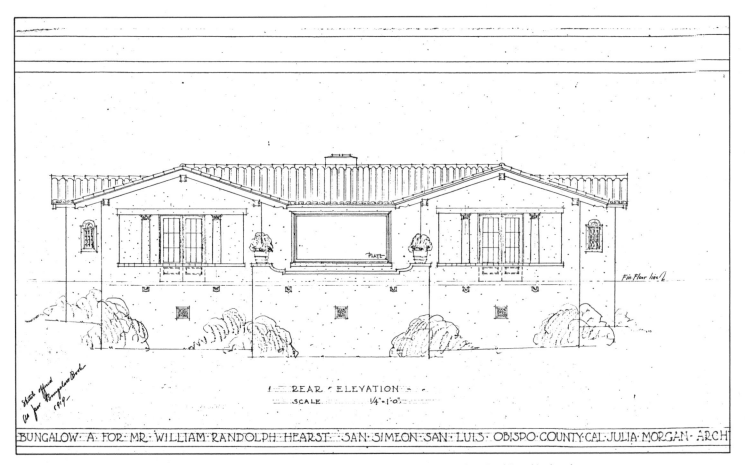

A Julia Morgan sketch for the Casa del Mar ("A" House) with a note which says ". . . as per Bungalow Book" and is dated
1919.

His Castle

The conversation with which this chapter opened continued, " . . . And the other day I was in a secondhand bookstore in Los Angeles just walking around as is my habit, and I came upon this booklet about bungalows and I don't want you to think that you're to follow this plan exactly but this gives you a general idea of the areas and so on that I would like. And it's this one. It is called the Swisso-Jappo bungalow." They both laughed heartily.

To be sure the house looked neither Swiss nor Japanese, but there is no reason to doubt the memory of Walter Steilberg who repeated the story a number of times in various interviews, both with the author, at the Castle, and for the oral history section of the Bancroft Library at Berkeley.

Drawings for "A" house or the Casa del Mar were started immediately in 1919. In 1920 drawings were prepared for "B" house or the Casa del Monte, and the following year for "C" house or the Casa del Sol. Preliminary drawings for a fourth house were prepared, but not used.

While working on the drawings for the first guest house Julia Morgan, giving rise to a flight of fancy, drew a tree-covered hilltop with three guest houses below, and a single tower rising above the billowing treetops against the sky. With variations the drawing was revised a number of times. One of the simple

sketches captured Mr. Hearst's imagination. Julia Morgan evidently realized a fatal "error" had been made. But it was too late. The twin tower idea was suitable for a cathedral or monastery, but it in no way suggested a country villa which, after all, was the intended use of the building. This supposition is borne out by the presence in drawing collections of numerous sketches attempting to reconcile the cathedral "look" with the residence "function". All to no avail. The finished facade of the Castle holds closely to the first sketch.

The second guest house, the Casa del Monte ("B" House) was started in 1920, and the third, the Casa del Sol ("C" House), a year later.

All the structures on the Hill were made of reinforced concrete, which was an unusual construction technique at the time, and covered with exterior cement plaster, stone, tile, or nothing, depending on the particular location. The cement was brought in sacks by boat from San Francisco and it was at first assumed that sand would have to be brought in also. Julia Morgan was fortunate. She had in her employ an engineer named Walter Steilberg, who had published technical articles and who had done experimental work in concrete. Mr. Steilberg visited the site and concluded that the sand and gravel mix available at the hill site would produce excellent

The facade showing the towers close together and a large second floor balcony.

concrete. The absence of cracking and the generally good condition of the concrete today, after half a century, indicate the accuracy of his assumption.

Such grading as was needed was accomplished by a steam shovel which was used jointly by the crews working in the gardens and the buildings.

Work continued on the Castle buildings from the early 1920s until 1937 when financial problems overtook the entire Hearst organization. During this period, sometime after 1927, in addition to other structures, the indoor Roman pool building with tennis court on top was under construction. The outdoor or Neptune Pool was built three times. A number of auxiliary structures, some made of wood and others of concrete, were needed to garage the cars, shelter the animals, and house the workmen.

Original drawings for the Casa Grande do not indicate a kitchen in back, let alone the theater and servants' quarters. These were added as the work on the front part of the Castle proceeded. Much later, in the brief years of Hearst's residency after World War II, the three floors of rooms over the theater were added. Warren McClure, a man who understood Miss Morgan's intentions, was engaged to do the design.

Changes in the drawings and construction were so frequent that no ''complete'' set of drawings for the Castle exists. There are additional drawings which indicate radical changes to pre-

sent buildings, possibly for dreams as yet unrealized.

The projects which were never erected include a grand staircase connecting the drive to the upper terrace on the north, a ballroom over the watertanks on the far hill to the south, and a possible cloister or a ballroom at the east end between the projecting arms.

The interiors of the towers, particularly the stairwells on the third and the fourth floor levels, are eloquent testimony to a tremendous amount of jackhammered concrete. Mr. Hearst, when touring the top of the Castle, ordered the remodeling to permit bedrooms to be constructed. The bedrooms needed a connection, so an additional gable was placed above the main roof to form a linking sitting room. This group of rooms became known as the Celestial Suite, the highest in the Castle. Arthur Brisbane, Hearst's right-hand man and virtual alter ego, presumably used the suite. Some reports claim that Mr. Hearst himself used the Celestial Suite, but this seems doubtful because his own quarters were immediately below.

The construction of the Castle differed from accepted practice in that the entire project was not conceived in advance either by architect Julia Morgan or client-architect William Randolph Hearst. Besides satisfying necessities such as eating, sleeping, sanitation, and social activities, and balancing such natural forces as gravity, orientation, wind, rain, and earthquakes, the spaces generated had to fit large-scale art objects,

La Casa Grande facade with square towers and a wide front.

Another study of the front elevation. The towers are treated as domes and the entrance is much more modest.

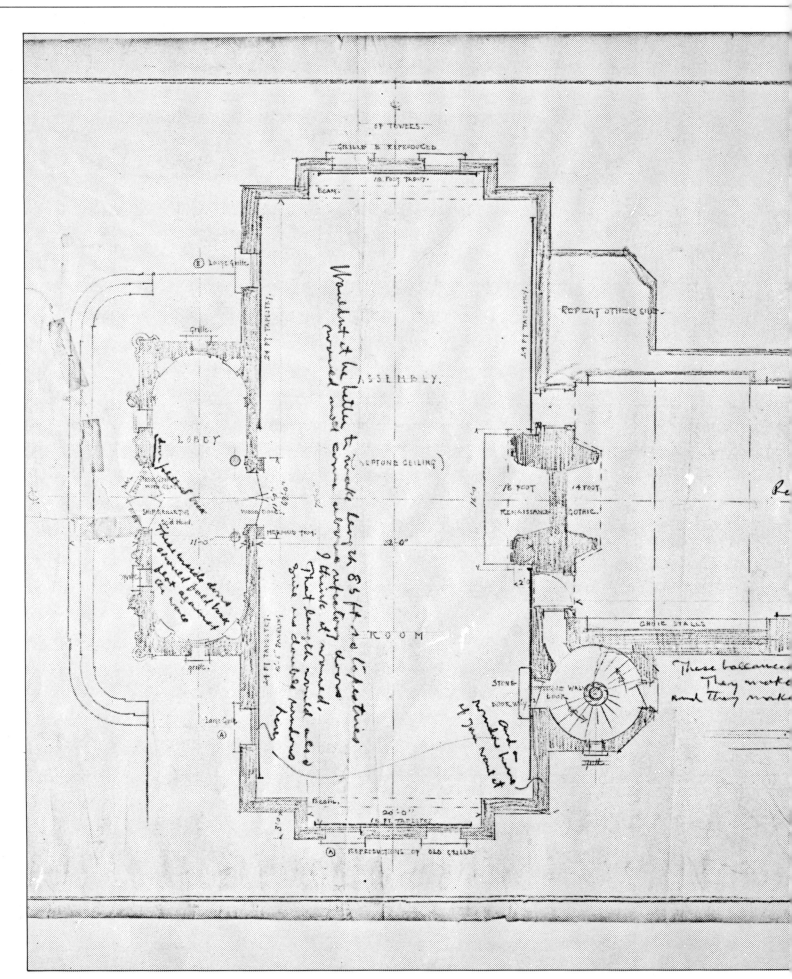

With minor adjustments, the first floor of La Casa Grande came to be laid out much as it appears in this early 1920s Julia Morgan drawing.

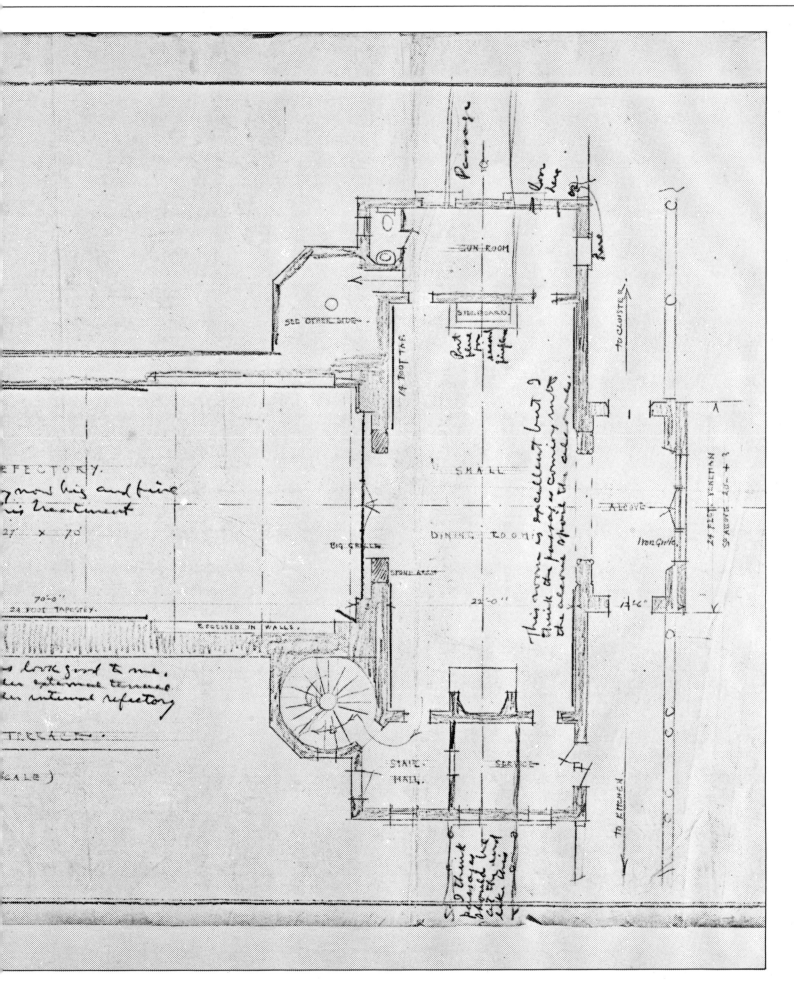

The facade of La Casa Grande under construction. The twin towers are yet to be completed.

The transplanting of native oaks to accommodate La Casa Grande required laborious and expensive techniques.

Five ton Italian cypresses were hauled to the hilltop one at a time from Paso Robles.

The construction of Casa del Sol ("C" House) in the early 1920s.

The citrus grove planted by Nigel Keep for William Randolph Hearst. The construction of the main building continues in the background.

Construction of the main reservoir on a hill just south of the Castle.

The construction of the Indoor Swimming Pool with the tennis court on the roof.

such as fireplaces, ceilings, tapestries, rugs, and wall paneling in the form of choir stalls, which Mr. Hearst had acquired and held in storage. Julia Morgan had the job of orchestrating the ensemble of Hearst's evolving requirements, functional needs, and the built-in artifacts and architectural components he continued to acquire. In addition, she had to keep construction moving and the cost within some limits.

The question is frequently asked about the effect of the art objects on the design of the Castle. An early drawing shows a floor plan with dark lines (red in the original). The drawing is by Julia Morgan or someone in her office. Handwriting by Mr. Hearst or someone else indicates that the Assembly Room must be made thirteen feet larger so the tapestries on the side walls would not hang over the doors to the Refectory or Dining Room. How often this demand was repeated is unknown, but it is certainly clear that at times the built-in art objects determined the design of the building.

According to Ken Murray, in his book *Golden Days of San Simeon,* Miss Morgan said, "Mr. Hearst and I are fellow architects. He supplies vision, critical judgment. I give technical knowledge and building experience. He loves architecturing. If he had chosen that career he would have been a great architect. San Simeon is Mr. Hearst."

The first outdoor swimming pool was removed and the Neptune Pool was constructed in its place.

The placement of the carillon bells in the towers. They were raised by rope, tripod
and manpower.

William Randolph Hearst with one of his dachshunds, Helen.

C H A P T E R   4

HEAVEN ON A HILLTOP

"Did Mr. Hearst keep his wife locked in the North Tower?" "Where was Marion Davies's room?" "Are there many undiscovered rooms in the Castle?" "Why did the guests not use the indoor Roman Pool?" "Were there secret passages leading from Mr. Hearst's quarters to various parts of the Castle?"

The answers to the above questions are for the most part "No." Yet they are asked repeatedly with every new tour group. Mystery and legend abound concerning life at the Castle. It is not necessary to invent stories. The facts are confounding enough in themselves.

What was a day like at Hearst Castle?

Charles Gibbs Adams, a landscape architect from Pasadena, mentioned in 1938 that evening meals were served at regular hours and you were expected to be on time. Failure to appear would evoke a note on your bed thanking you for coming, but indicating that your room was now needed for another person. Mr. Adams says that Mr. Hearst loved to eavesdrop on conversations in the Assembly Room prior to dinner. Many such remarks surprised many a guest in one of Mr. Hearst's newspapers the next day.

In writing this chapter about life at the Castle, we can point to very little accurate documentation, but when various stories from independent sources are repeated, we can safely assume they are close to the truth. What follows then is a carefully considered reconstruction.

Certainly a major function, if not the prime function, of the

Mr. Hearst swimming in the Neptune Pool.

Enchanted Hill — the landscape, pool, gardens, trails, zoo, and vast collections of art objects — was the entertainment, amusement, and bewilderment of guests, a fact which supports the Resort Theory of the Castle. But the Castle was not a continuous independent environment. It had a limited life of its own. When Mr. Hearst was not at the Castle, the staff was generally with him and all but the necessary activities ceased.

The method of selecting guests is uncertain, but was probably worked out between Mr. Hearst and Marion Davies. The length of an individual's stay also fluctuated. Some people remained for a long weekend or merely overnight, while others stayed several weeks.

Those who visited the Castle were as varied as were Mr. Hearst's collections. One wonders if the guests were merely temporary additions to his permanent collection. Politicians, newspapermen, actors and actresses, authors, comedians, sports figures, notables of the day, and relatives all came to eat, sleep, play, and enjoy themselves at the Enchanted Hill. The following random list of visitors to the Castle illustrates that Mr. Hearst's acquaintances stretched far and wide. Visitors to the Ranch, as he preferred the Castle to be called, included Mayor Jimmy Walker of New York, President and Mrs. Calvin Coolidge, Arthur Brisbane, Adela Rogers St. Johns, Robert Montgomery, Douglas Fairbanks Jr., Marie Dressler, Robert Taylor, Dolores del Rio, Cary Grant, Joan Crawford,

Bernard Shaw, Charles "Charlie" Chaplin, Charles Farrell, Bill Tilden, Charles Lindberg, A.P. Giannini (head of Bank of America), and Arthur and Pat Lake. (She was Marion Davies's niece.)

Invitations were sometimes extended by one of Mr. Hearst's secretaries by phone or by telegram, as in this reply to San Francisco publisher John Henry Nash to visit the Ranch: "Letter received, Mr. Hearst will be very happy to have you visit (the) Ranch with Mrs. Nash and friends you mentioned at the time stated. Have notified Ranch." The reply is signed by J. Willicombe, who was Colonel Joseph Willicombe, secretary to Mr. Hearst for a number of years.

Guests were transported to the Castle by various means, usually by train from Los Angeles. During the 1930s, a private train left Glendale station around 7:30 P.M. and arrived in San Luis Obispo near midnight. Steve Zegar, who passed away only recently in San Luis Obispo, owned a fleet of cars and provided transportation to and from the Castle. A private landing strip is still in use, adjacent to the Ranch buildings below the Castle. It was used occasionally by guests. However, it was most frequently used by Mr. Hearst. Some people arrived in their own cars, particularly when arriving during mid-week.

Ilka Chase, in her book *Past Imperfect,* writes of her second visit to San Simeon. "Mother and I set off in my car. It is a beautiful drive; the last thirty miles of the road borders the Hearst property, and as we turned in at the unpretentious wooden gates and started the seven mile drive to the house, we passed hundreds of wooden boxes scattered on the beach which held the ancient Spanish monastery Hearst had had torn down and imported from Europe with some vague idea of reassembling it under the California sky."

The prime mode of transportation preferred by Mr. Hearst in the 1920s was chauffeurred limousines. The guests assembled at the Ambassador Hotel in Los Angeles and, after being assigned to a car, they were driven in a procession up the coast to San Simeon.

However one arrived at San Simeon, the drive up the hill was taken by car. The road used today is little changed. Most weekend guests who drove along the Coast Highway and arrived at night could see the floodlighted twin towers from miles away.

The road up the hill, (which is five miles long, not seven as Ilka Chase states), had gates and guard houses at several points along the way. The location of the Castle itself discouraged unexpected guests. And an invitation was a requirement for admittance onto Hearst land. Once admitted and past the main gate, one entered William Randolph Hearst's version of a fairytale.

A guest was immediately transported to a different world. Large signs stating "ALWAYS DRIVE SLOWLY — ANIMALS HAVE THE RIGHT OF WAY" were discernible even in the fog which sometimes shrouds the lower portions of the hills. Along the road there were areas for large grazing animals, the antelope,

Mr. Hearst playing croquet.

deer, bison, elk, mountain sheep and zebras, as well as areas for special animals such as the giraffes and water buffaloes. Hearst had the world's largest private zoo and game preserve, which included over 120 varieties of animals housed on the hilltop, representing both grazing and carnivorous types.

Before arrival, guests were assigned rooms, but the exact method of making assignments is unknown. Usually the guests were met by the housekeeper, who escorted them to their rooms, answered any questions, and planned for their comfort.

Certain rooms were sometimes identified with particular guests. Mr. Hearst's wife, on her rare visits west, presumably used the Doge's Suite. Adela Rogers St. Johns claims to have been quartered in the Doge's Suite as well, except on her first visit when she stayed in one of the bungalows because Mrs. Hearst was present. Colonel Willicombe appears to have been the occupant of the rather plain room directly over the Billiard Room. Marion Davies used the North Bedroom of the Gothic Suite on the floor over the library, and Arthur Brisbane used the Celestial Suite, presumably built for him. Beyond this, rooms undoubtedly were assigned as space was available.

Life at the Castle adhered to a definite schedule. Breakfast was served between 9:00 A.M. and 11:00 A.M. and was available to the guests when they chose to appear. Room service was not encouraged except in case of illness. Fruit, juice and coffee were available in the Refectory, to be enjoyed while ordering individual breakfasts from the butler or one of his assistants. The morning meal was cooked to order and served hot from the kitchen. The only exception to the rule of breakfast in the Refectory appears to be Mr. Hearst himself. His valet prepared a tray for him around 10:00 A.M. consisting of juice, coffee, and toast with crab apple jelly, served in his private suite.

Lunch appeared at about 1:30 P.M. and was also informal, but guests were expected to be prompt as lunch was usually served buffet style in the Morning Room. A brass cow bell rang to announce the meal. The dishes and platters were placed on electric warmers. Mr. Hearst and his guests would file by and select their own food.

Since transportation to and from the hilltop was difficult, guests tended to stay right there. During the afternoon hours there were any number of diversions. Walking about the gardens, riding Arabian horses selected from Mr. Hearst's stable, playing tennis, swimming in the Neptune or in the Roman pool, reading one of 9,000 volumes housed in two libraries were all available for entertainment at the Castle. The equipment and clothing necessary to enjoy any sport or recreation was also available on request. Use of the facilities was encouraged and was frequently stimulated by the host's involvement.

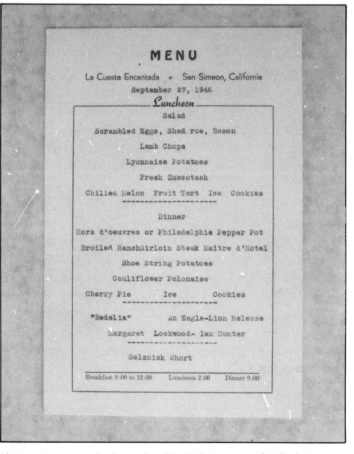

A page from La Casa Grande's guest book.

Feeding the animals in the zoo was, of course, a daily activity and evidently enjoyed by both Mr. Hearst and the guests. Behind La Casa Grande was a large circular area with pie-shaped sections containing some of the more unusual animals, both carnivores and primates from Hearst's collection. Each of the cages led into a central viewing and feeding area, where an individual animal could be admitted and viewed to better advantage. In the afternoon the lions, tigers, chimpanzees, and other zoo inhabitants were fed and observed by Mr. Hearst and his guests.

When Richard Addison, the first zoo keeper at the hilltop, was asked to explain why Mr. Hearst collected such a variety of animals, he said, "It was because of his fondness for them, maybe as a little boy's love for his pets. It wasn't just for show or part of the setting; he actually liked those creatures and was always concerned for their comfort."

Some animals had names such as Mary Ann, the elephant; Goofus, a bear; Slobbers, a camel; and Cassey, a cassowary. Birds were raised for the table and carrier pigeons were trained to carry messages from the Castle to the cattle ranch headquarters near Jolon. Down the hill from the Castle were the cages for the bears, a short walk on a warm afternoon.

Mr. Hearst himself would mingle with the guests for short periods of time or longer, depending on the demands of the moment. Certain activities interested him greatly, especially

MENU

La Cuesta Encantada ◆ San Simeon, California
September 27, 1946

Luncheon

Salad

Scrambled Eggs, Shad roe, Bacon

Lamb Chops

Lyonnaise Potatoes

Fresh Zuccotash

Chilled Melon   Fruit Tart   Ice   Cookies

Dinner

Hors d'oeuvres or Philadelphia Pepper Pot

Broiled Ranch Sirloin Steak Maitre d'Hotel

Shoe String Potatoes

Cauliflower Polonaise

Cherry Pie   Ice   Cookies

"Bedelia"   An Eagle-Lion Release

Margaret Lockwood- Ian Hunter

Selznick Short

Breakfast 9:00 to 12:00   Luncheon 2:00   Dinner 9:00

The luncheon menu for September 27, 1946. A guest at the Castle was expected to attend all meals and the evening movie.

The Hearsts entertained the famous. Here Phoebe Apperson Hearst is shown with Thomas Alva Edison.

MENU

La Cuesta Encantada ✦ San Simeon, California

December 25, 1946

Dinner

LOBSTER TERMADORE

ROAST TURKEY - DRESSING - CRANBERRY SAUCE

MASHED POTATOES   STRING BEANS

PLUM-PUDDING HARD SAUCE BRANDY SAUCE

ICE CREAM   CAKE

* * * * * * * * * *

PICTURE:

"THE GOLDDIGGERS OF 1937," WITH DICK

POWELL AND JOAN BLONDELL", FROM WARNER

BROS. STUDIO.

SHORT FROM WARNER BROS. STUDIO.

NEWSREELS FROM MGM EXCHANGE

Breakfast 9:00 to 12:00   Luncheon 2:00   Dinner 9:00

The dinner menu for September 26, 1946.

planning the Castle with Julia Morgan. When she was in residence, social obligations were put aside so that he could devote his undivided attention to her and her drawings. She routinely sat next to him at dinner with Marion Davies across the table.

Dinner was served at 8:30 or 9:00 P.M. and all the guests were expected to be on hand. Absence would be checked since placecards were used. The guests would gather at around 7:00 in what is now known as the Assembly Room. (It was then called by another name, according to Adela Rogers St. Johns.) The guests might amuse themselves by playing the grand piano or indulging in any one of the numerous games provided, such as bingo, cards, monopoly, Chinese checkers or dominoes.

Mr. Hearst would not be on hand when the guests arrived for dinner as might be expected, but would drop down in the private elevator from the Gothic Suite above the Library around 8:00 P.M. He would appear as if by magic through the choir stalls, usually accompanied not by glamorous women, but by at least two dachshunds, who would run wildly about the Assembly Room leaping on furniture and guests alike.

Mr. Hearst would move from group to group greeting the multitude and, depending on the talent available, strains of "Yes, We Have No Bananas" and "Here Comes Barney Google, With His Goo Goo Googly Eyes" would be heard

Mr. Hearst, Marion Davies, and an assortment of executives and movie stars in Civil War costumes for a typical extravagant party.

from the south end of the room where the piano was located.

When the staff was ready, dinner was announced by the butler. The guests moved from the Assembly Room to the Refectory or Dining Room through concealed panels or doors on either side of the massive fireplace to search the table for their placecards.

The organization of the placecards was extremely important and this responsibility was discharged by Marion Davies. Proximity to the host and hostess was based on some arbitrary measure of importance, but length of stay was also a factor. Guests who had been around for some time might find themselves sitting toward either end of the table and could take the broad hint that it was time to leave. Mr. Hearst sat on the north side of the great table, with Miss Davies directly opposite. Those to the left or right of the host or hostess were in high regard at the moment.

Ludwig Bemelmans, in his book *To The One I Love The Best,* describes his first impressions of the Refectory:

"I walked through the dining hall. It is formidable Gothic. Up above hang the old, torn battle flags of the city of Siena. Below is a table the length of the room, so big that whoever sits at the far end is very small. Here again is a fireplace that devours the trunks of trees. The flames, behind a glass screen, leap up to the height of a man. At the right is an armorer's anvil, arresting and beautiful, but the base of it is fixed to hold nuts, and on top of the anvil lies a hammer to crack the nuts. There are tall silver altar candlesticks all along

the center of the long refectory table, and between them stand, in a straight line and in repeating pattern, bottles of catsup, chili sauce, pickled peaches, A-1 sauce, salt and pepper in shakers that are cute little five-and-ten-cent figures of Donald Duck with silvered porcelain feet, and glasses in which are stuck a handful of paper napkins."

Wine was served with dinner. It seems quite reliable that two drinks per person was the accepted limit before dinner, with the possibility of a highball after. On occasion Roy Rogers and the Sons of the Pioneers appeared, somewhat incongruously, in the music gallery of the Refectory, to serenade Mr. Hearst and his guests with such popular hits as "Tumbling Tumbleweeds."

Dinner was served by some of the kitchen staff, the butler and/or his assistants. Dinner usually started with a hearty soup, such as terrapin Maryland, turtle soup, or lentil soup. The main course followed, served with potatoes and a vegetable. Mr. Hearst preferred fowl, lamb, corned beef and ham to steak. Occasionally beef, kidneys, or tripe was served. Pressed duck, a favorite of the host, was roasted for only twelve minutes with a sauce made of the blood and juices extracted when the duck was pressed. And desserts included cakes, pie and pastries, puddings, fruit, and specialties such as boiled apple dumplings and fresh lemon sherbet.

After dinner a newly released motion picture would be shown in the Theater. Flown in from the "Film Capitol," they

Mr. Hearst and Pancho Estrada, a descendant of an early California family, often rode together on the San Simeon Ranch.

began around 11:00 P.M. The staff would attempt to finish the washing up in time to see the movie, but on occasion, according to one eye witness, Marion Davies would substitute one of her own celluloids at the end of the first reel and the help would quietly vanish from the Theater. Usually the films were the latest releases or yet to be released MGM movies. The fifty-seat theater is reputed to be the first place to show the newly completed, soon-to-be legendary *Gone With The Wind,* possibly six months before its premiere on December 14, 1939. Mr. Hearst sat in a big silk upholstered chair on the aisle, conveniently close to his telephone to talk to the projectionist or, through his own switchboard, to any of the far-flung businesses of his empire.

Following the movie, the guests would converse a bit, enjoy a quick game of pool or billiards, or play cards before departing for their respective quarters.

The logistics for supplying the needs of thirty to fifty guests were not as complex as Versailles Palace at the time of Louis IV, where 5,000 inhabitants could be accommodated. Still, the problem had to be met and food supply demanded considerable attention. Some food was purchased in San Luis Obispo, with more exotic fare flown in from Young's Market in Los Angeles or from San Francisco. The special requests and desires, allegedly of Marion Davies, were catered to by air freight from one of the major urban centers.

Mr. Hearst supplied his guests with basic toilet articles and some medicine, since drugstores were not convenient. The daily papers were driven up, leaving Los Angeles at 3:00 A.M. and arriving in time for breakfast.

It would appear that an expedition to the Castle had come a long way from the rough campsite excursion it once was. The Castle had become a unique "resort hotel," where everything was free, except the phone bill.

Nature provided this human splendor with a magnificent setting and an isolated peace. One still senses it. And even now while the visitor stands on one of the many balconies gazing at the landscape, he might hear the ghost-like tinkle of glasses and silverware, or a muted voice rising in a burst of laughter, or a piano and tenor singing "Ain't She Sweet."

"Crouching Venus," a modern reproduction by an unknown sculptor, graces the South Court of Casa del Monte.

C H A P T E R 5

THE POOLS, THE GARDENS AND THE OUTDOOR SCULPTURE

Mr. Hearst had a large front yard. The Castle is five miles away from the Pacific Ocean and 1600 feet above it. His back-yard was even larger. It consisted of 250,000 acres, plus or minus. In 1940, 164,000 acres were sold to the War Department. The land became the Hunter-Liggit Military Reserve. Still, this left him with 75,000 acres, slightly more than the original three Mexican Land Grants which constituted George Hearst's original holdings. From the crest of the hill where the Castle begins, the Hearst lands roll away to the East, North, and South.

As if the natural beauty of the place — the sea, the mountains, and the sun, embellished by natural flora and fauna — were not enough, Mr. Hearst added both animals and plants

of his own choosing. At one time, there were seventy varieties of grazing animals and thirty varieties of meat-eating animals. The animals on the hilltop included an elephant, tigers, water buffaloes, yak, ostriches, and chimpanzees. Some had to be kept in cages while others were allowed to roam selected areas.

Besides those caged animals mentioned previously, the grazing animals also had housing. Shelters and feeding stations were built close to the road and were made of logs, which were notched and chinked like a log cabin. Tall structures were built for the giraffes, and single-story structures for most other animals. Chain-link fenced areas restrained unruly or pregnant animals. Those who were perpetual malcontents were kept away from the roads and the Castle, confined to an area known as "Devil's Island." A crew of people was employed just to collect and grow the foods needed for the animals. Mr. Hearst raised Arabian horses and dachshunds. About seventy to eighty long- and short-haired dachshunds and Kerry Blue terriers were kenneled behind La Casa Grande. He was always kind to the animals, but wanted them visible to the guests.

The animals for the Zoo came from abroad and were purchased from such famous collections as Carl Hagenback of German circus fame and Shultz of East Africa. Mr. Addison, the first zoo keeper, describes his initial interview with Mr. Hearst: "We discussed the types of animals which would or wouldn't thrive in the San Simeon climate and terrain, and I found that he (Mr. Hearst) knew quite a bit about wild animals, their natures, and the requirements for keeping them healthy and contented under semi-confinement."

Many wonder whether any of the zoo animals from Mr. Hearst's time are still in the area. Most visitors will get a chance to see part of what is growing into a rather considerable herd of zebras as they are driven up and down the hill in the tour buses. The zebras actually belong to a private individual who, through arrangements with the Hearst Corporation, has been keeping his animals on the ranch for several years now. Even though the herd is not directly descended from the zebras of the original zoo, the impression is that they are, and everyone enjoys imagining for a moment that this segment of the old Hearst zoo lives on. The zebras have multiplied: each year has produced its share of new colts, scampering about the hills in their fuzzy brown stripes (the black and white look develops with age). A couple of wooly yaks had been put out to pasture on the ranch by the zebras' owner, but they have since been removed.

Meanwhile, some of the animals from Mr. Hearst's time *are* still to be seen today, although much less frequently than the zebras, which seem to be quite accustomed to bus and car traffic on the hill. A large herd of aoudad, or Barbary sheep, can be spotted from time to time—in fact these rather wild, scruffy looking yet noble creatures sometimes hold up hilltop traffic long enough for a good two or three hundred of them to make their crossing! This is something witnessed pretty much only by those who work at the Castle on a regular basis and thus drive up and down the hill everyday, but once in awhile visitors riding in the tour buses are treated to a view of the aoudad herd.

Also descended from the original wild animal park are the tahr goats of Himalayan origin. Like the aoudads, the tahrs constitute a rather sizeable herd. They mostly stay out of view, although the formation locally known as Goat Rock seems to be a favorite tramping ground of theirs. Goat Rock can be seen off the right of the roadway about halfway down the hill from the Castle. Look carefully toward Goat Rock as you pass the old giraffe shelters (identifiable by their great height) and

you might spot a few of the tahrs picking their way up and down the slopes of the rock with the greatest of ease.

A herd of Roosevelt elk usually stays toward the back country east and north of the Enchanted Hill and can be seen at times through a pair of binoculars if you know just where to look. This counts out the average visitor, but down in the canyon that parallels the road to the Castle can be seen a few sambar deer from India, which are just as impressive as the Roosevelt elk. The sambar are visible most days provided the visitor knows where to look. Be ready to look down into the canyon right after the bus rounds the first big turn past the Poultry Ranch and starts up the long, gradual straightaway to the middle part of the hill slope below the Castle. Off to the right and down in the canyon is where you should look to spot these animals. They are usually seen in the small, open patches of hillside that appear between the larger stretches of dense undergrowth and chaparral. The sambar deer are a kind of dark reddish brown color and will look almost black from a distance.

Stories are heard of wild boar, African oryx and pygmy goat, and other types of wild animals that escaped from the zoo confines during Mr. Hearst's era and have since gone into the nearby wilderness on their own. Few if any animals of this type are ever seen. The area's native species are interesting enough in their own right. Coastal deer are a very common sight. Less frequently seen, but by no means nonexistent, are fox, bobcat, coyote, and, soaring overhead, the handsome red-tail hawk. Mountain lion appears to be as good as extinct in this region today, although stories of their living in the most remote reaches of the lower Big Sur–San Simeon area are still told. Bear were common a century or so ago, but they have vanished without a trace.

The natural hillsides around the Castle were almost treeless. California Live Oak (Quercus Agrifolia) grew on the ridges. There were five other varieties of oak growing in the arroyos and valleys. Mr. Hearst did not care for the bare ridges and hilltops and some twenty-four varieties of conifers were planted in the vicinity of the Castle. These included cypress, cedar, spruce, pine, yew, redwood, and Giant Sequoia. In many places the earth on the hilltop was too hard for manual digging and thousands of dynamite charges were used to create the basins for the trees. Thousands of tons of planting soil were trucked in to make raised beds and to fill thousands of holes blown into the San Simeon rock for the trees and large bushes.

Some trees were brought in full grown. For example, thirty-three Italian cypress belonging to Mr. Claasen of Paso Robles were purchased by Mr. Hearst in 1928. They were not moved and transplanted until some years later. Palms from Berkeley and a beautiful fan palm from the Dickey place in Harmony, California were transplanted to the hilltop site. Nearly fifty varieties of fruit and citrus trees were planted close to the house,

The Neptune Pool provides a perfect setting for a reconstructed temple from ancient Italy. Columns are of granite, and entablature and roof sections are marble; Neptune and two nereids occupy the pediment.

Fine Arabian horses have been raised for many years at the Pico Creek Stables on the Hearst Ranch.

including orange, avocado, and grapefruit. More exotic varieties of fruit were grown, such as loquat, kumquat, lime quince, and persimmon. In addition, about 130 varieties of ornamental trees can be found somewhere on the hilltop.

Not only were the hill running westward from the Castle and the opposite Reservoir Hill landscaped in Mr. Hearst's time, but various spots close to the Castle, as well as quite far away from it, were planted during the 1920s and 30s too, although not nearly on the scale mentioned above. In one area a big grove of Canary Pines is clustered on a cone-shaped knob halfway between the coastal plain and the hilltop itself; this can be seen off to the right of the uphill half of the roadway, about two miles from the Visitor Center. Back of the Castle, down in the canyon and visible from the north side of the Hill is said to be a small grove of Sequoia Gigantea. Few can claim to have seen this remarkable bit of ornamental horticulture on the grand scale — only those who were guests at the Castle during its heyday, and those who are guests of the Hearst family of today and can take a jeep or horseback ride to the spot where the trees stand.

The road to the Castle follows the original trail that led from the center of the ranch to the campsite. After boarding the bus the visitor sees a number of interesting sights on the ride to the Castle. A grove of Eucalyptus trees on the left conceals the delightful Victorian house built by George Hearst for his

wife and son. Farther along on the right side is a building designed by Julia Morgan. The architecture is Mission or Spanish Colonial Revival and it functioned as the poultry farm headquarters. The building is in a lovely setting and is a good example of the type of structure Miss Morgan designed many times. The headquarters building, at Jolon, is similar but larger and more distinguished in appearance.

The hills appear much as they did when George Hearst first acquired the land, except for the groves of trees in the ridge adjacent to the Castle. On another hill to the South, a round water reservoir with a capacity of 1,250,000 gallons is now concealed by planted trees. This tank is fed by a spring from a peak called Pine Mountain, 2,000 feet above the Castle. The tank in turn siphons water into two copper 2,500 gallon tanks high in the Castle towers. Today this water system supplies the intensive use of the visitors' center and, interestingly, the water continued to flow, with certain restrictions, during a recent drought.

The slope and brow of the hill near the Castle is covered with pines planted by a crew under the direction of Nigel Keep. Mr. Keep, an Englishman, was engaged by Julia Morgan to plant and care for the extensive grounds and the Enchanted Hill. Besides designing the building and working as the on-site contractor, Miss Morgan engaged most of the staff for Mr. Hearst. Not only did she employ the construction crew, but

"Naissance de Venus" (Birth of Venus) was executed by the Parisian sculptor Charles Cassou in the late 1920s. The group is located in a square-shaped alcove at the Neptune Pool.

One of Charles Cassou's marble groups representing "Leda and the Swan" (Neptune Pool).

she also hired the zoo keepers, Mr. Richard Addison and Mr. Carey Baldwin; the head grounds man, Nigel Keep; the head flower gardener, Mr. Macklen, a Scot; and one of the house-keepers, Mrs. O'Brien, a Canadian.

Later, Mr. Addison, when writing about work at the Castle, said about Julia Morgan: "The Miss Morgan who had signed the telegram turned out to be a slightly built little person, the architect who had designed the fabulous castle that Mr. Hearst was building, and who also had hired all the employees there, the engineers, gardeners, landscapers, horticulturists, stone masons, artisans, etc. . . ."

Where it nears the top of the hill, the road up to the Castle is bordered with oleander trimmed in an unusual way with foliage at the top and bottom to allow an unobstructed view through the middle. A seemingly endless arbor of cement posts and wood beams lies along the edge of the ridge giving it the appearance of a recumbent snake sunning itself. The pergola, as it is called, is a mile-long bridle trail. It begins and ends near the same spot, and is also used as support for the grape vines, and espaliered fruit trees. Its delapidated appearance today is not due to negligence on the part of the California State Parks Department. The property which the trail covers is still owned by the Hearst Corporation.

By the time we emerge from the grove of pines adjacent to the Castle, we are close to the structure; but what we see is

Emperor Hadrian's Tivoli . . .

the back side of the huge wall from which horizontal concrete beams extend to the retaining wall of the Neptune Pool at the upper slope. Plant varieties have now multiplied at the top and bottom of this wall. In addition to the native Coast Live Oak, we find Andora Juniper, bougainvillea, California golden privet, Canary Island pine, citrus, cottoneaster, eugenia, grewia, poinsettia, pomegranate, pyracantha, and Spanish broom.

The problem of a main entrance to the Castle was never resolved. The unfinished grand staircase in the Garden, in fact, would still not have resolved the problem. How Mr. Hearst's guests, family, and tradesmen approached the building remains a puzzle.

Since there was no formal entrance to the Castle, it looks as though most guests were driven along the present roadway, passing the spot where the tours now disembark, and they continued on around the Indoor Pool to the south side of the Hill to a small cul-de-sac. They were escorted up a short flight of stairs to the South Terrace above and then proceeded to the Main Terrace, one level higher still. However satisfactory an approach this may have been — so far as practicality and proximity to the Castle was concerned — it couldn't possibly provide the kind of impact that walking up a grand flight of steps to the North Terrace would have made if the Grand Entrance had been finished. In stormy weather or in the case of nighttime arrivals, guests were driven right up to the back of

. . . and the pool of a latter-day Hadrian.

Paul Manaut's "La Source," a sculpture group in the Moderne style of the 1920s.

South colonnade, the Neptune Pool.

the Castle, where they entered the building through the Morning Room from the big back courtyard. Whichever method was used, there were a number of servants to carry the baggage and to show the guests to their quarters, where they would be made to feel at home right away.

The visitor is taken to the Neptune Pool and La Casa Grande by a variety of routes, depending on the specific tour. The lower portions of the planted areas flank the guest houses and surround the terraces below each. Some of these areas are not visible on tour, but the upper portions are contained by the guest houses and the Esplanade, which links the smaller buildings and terraces and which surrounds La Casa Grande like a giant necktie. The Esplanade in fact follows the undisturbed contours of the original hill. Extensive grading was impossible. To his everlasting credit, Mr. Hearst respected plants and trees and refused to allow the native oaks to be removed.

Several mature oak trees were moved under the direction of Nigel Keep. In 1922, a large oak, located where the main terrace and the statue of "Galatea on the Dolphin" were to be placed, was moved fifty feet west. In 1947, another oak was moved twelve feet to the east of the kitchen.

Live oak trees, even though they grow to be huge and stately, can deteriorate quickly if the hand of man gets too close. An oak, which has stood for a couple of hundred years

Giovanni Bologna's fountain at the Villa Petraia, Tuscany, is the model for two such fountains at San Simeon.

One of many light standards inspired by a Graeco-Roman boundary marker.

A copy of Donatello's "David" stands atop a marble and limestone fountain in front of La Casa del Sol.

in one spot, can succumb to overwatering if ornamental plants, which require large quantities of water, are placed too close by. Through long droughts as well as through the occasionally very wet winters, the old oaks stand their ground—they seem to be destined to live forever. But place a few small plants too close, or put a concrete walkway or retaining wall near their sensitive root systems, and the threat of a quick and irreversible death of the trees looms ominously. Many Californians who have moved into new suburban developments where oaks remain from more rural times have found this out; even on the Enchanted Hill a few oaks have met a premature doom for such reasons. So fragile are these giants, and so highly regarded are they as garden specimens, that number-tags have been attached to them. In this way Norman Rotanzi (who has been at the Castle since 1934) and his staff of groundsmen keep records on them. If some tree surgery is needed, or if a tree is showing signs of undue decay, a note is made in the records alongside the appropriate number: a complete tree-history is maintained. Visitors marvel at the big trees with good reason. Many visitors notice the elaborate system of guy-wires that seem to help hold the trees together, limb by limb. The wires are there not only to keep the limbs from breaking off because of old age or the stress of winter storms, but also to minimize damage to whatever is below—plants, walkways and retaining walls (and even passerby) should one of the enormous limbs come crashing down, as they have been known to do on occasion. Considering all this it seems even more amazing that any of these trees could ever have been moved successfully in the first place.

The terrain on the hilltop precluded a geometrically patterned, formal garden design like those the French cultivated at Versailles or Vaux le Vicomte. Symmetry is not a Castle conscious design attribute. Even the guest houses are not placed symmetrically around the Great House partly because they were placed to take advantage of specific views and partly because a master plan emerged after the fact as the work progressed. The three guest houses are all single story, on the uphill side, and extend down the hill for additional stories.

Casa del Mar ("A" House) gives the impression from the west side of being a four or five story building. Actually it consists of only two interior stories plus a separate lower area that evidently was a servants' quarters years ago. From the back, or Esplanade side, the building appears to be only one story high. The reason for this is because the hill slope is so steep that a foundation had to be notched into the hillside. Casa del Monte ("B" House) and Casa del Sol ("C" House) have similar foundations, but they don't extend down the hillside quite as far as "A" House. Casa del Monte looks like a two-story structure but, in reality, has just one floor with an unfinished basement space beneath. (There is a theory that this basement space was to be converted into a lower story of finished interior rooms eventually.) Casa del Sol is the only one of the three

A modern copy of the "Nike of Brescia" by Umberto Marcellini, Naples, Italy.

houses where outside appearance, down the hillside, actually corresponds to the actual amount of interior space. These variances in the three guest houses stem from individual considerations of the building site at hand. The plot-plan of the Enchanted Hill is big enough so that we can think of it as consisting of several individual building sites within the master plan. This siting—the cluster of the three bungalows surrounding the main house and all the buildings situated on top of hill—gives us not only a spectacular view but also a masterful use of the natural environment.

Moving north or west to the Neptune Pool area, depending upon the tour, we encounter one of the most beautiful outdoor spaces on the Hill. The swimming pool itself was enlarged twice after its original construction. The original pool was a clover-shaped Beverly Hills style pool, complete with patio and palm trees. It was large for a pool, but nowhere near the size it is now.

On the northwest side of the pool is a fragment of a Roman temple with the triangular pediment containing a Renaissance sculpture. The sculpture group includes Neptune, minus his trident, and two nereids. In fact, the whole temple fragment appears to be an assemblage of parts from different locations, but the detail of the carving is very well done and has the appearance of an authentic Roman fragment.

Neptune was the chief of the water deities. The symbol of

High relief Roman sarcophagus of the Nine Muses. This photograph was taken about 1930.

"The Wrestlers" in Carrara marble (Romanelli Brothers, Florence, Italy).

his power was the trident, a spear with three points. He used his trident to shatter rocks, to call forth or subdue storms, to shape the shores to his will. We hope that this Neptune has not lost his power by being deprived of his trident. The two figures who share the pediment with Neptune are nereids, the daughters of Nereus and his wife Doris. The nereids also inhabited the water world.

The south side of the pool contains numerous sculptured mermaids and mermen swimming in the water, and swans with cupids and/or putti on their backs. A basin of water at the next level contains a statue of the "Birth of Venus," the Goddess of love, born from the sea foam. Above this statue there was planned a statue of Neptune driving a chariot pulled by horses, but this work was badly broken in transit to the United States and was never replaced. The seven carved Carrara marble statuary groups around the pool and in the alcove are by French sculptor Charles Cassou. Most are dated 1929 and 1930, and were done in Paris.

The semicircular colonnades at either end of the Neptune Pool were designed by Julia Morgan. The colonnades are made of white marble fabricated in Vermont and assembled on the hilltop site. The four rectangular reliefs mounted on the walls of the colonnade are probably sixteenth or seventeenth century Italian bas-reliefs showing poets and philosophers of the classical world.

Detail of a bench support by H. Petrilli of Florence, Italy.

Sensuous "Galatea" is the focal point of the Main Terrace.

The pool terrace itself occupies a stunning location. The south end commands a view of the coastline in a great sweeping arc, while from the north end the tops of trees in the foreground lead the eye to the distant hills, still part of the ranch. The semicircular colonnades at either end enclose the space without confining the viewer.

The pool itself is one hundred and four feet long, with a graduated depth of three feet six inches to ten feet. The pool has a capacity of 345,000 gallons. Water is channeled from the natural springs in Pine Mountain to a holding tank of 100,000 gallons, then to a second tank holding 1,200,000 gallons. The system is gravity flow so the Castle never has to depend on a pump for its water supply. The large room below the pool contains an elaborate filter system which uses pure sand as a filtering agent.

The bottom and sides of the pool are faced with white Vermont marble with a grid design made of a dark green marble called Verde Antique. Around the pool are lamp standards made of cast concrete in the shops on the hilltop. They represent a Greco Roman Herm and were copied from a marble original which is found in the Library in La Casa Grande. (A herm is a statue in the form of a square stone pillar surmounted by a bust or head, especially of Hermes [Mercury]. In mythology Hermes was the son of Jupiter and Maia. He presided over commerce, wrestling, and other gymnastic exer-

cises. He even presided over thieving and everything requiring skill and dexterity.) The lamp standards are approximately one third larger than the original. The Hermes are topped by glass balls over the light bulbs. The original fixtures were alabaster which is thin and brittle. The strong winds and storms on the hilltop took a toll on these fixtures. The State of California has replaced them with glass, but a few of alabaster remain on lamp standards directly in front of La Casa Grande and in the Indoor Swimming Pool. Even during Mr. Hearst's time the fixtures were being replaced.

It is fascinating to note that, for all its size and weight, a goodly portion of the Neptune Pool is actually situated *above* ground level. This is mainly due to the steepness of the hillside on which the pool rests. The subterranean space which is located near the shallow end of the pool is so considerable that there is enough room to house the extensive filtering and plumbing system. Walking around under the colonnades and to the end of the pool where the equipment is located, reminds one of being in the engine room of some great ocean liner. Pipes, valves, gauges, pumps, and other equipment are tangled together in a wonderfully functional maze of rather ultra-modern machinery; curiously modern, if one considers the antique look of the swimming pool area just a short distance above. Other instances of the architectural and engineering skill of Julia Morgan can be found, but the handling

Madelaine Fessard's ''Girl with Parrot.''

Italian cypresses and palms near the North Terrace.

of the Neptune Pool ''problem'' is about as impressive an example as can be found anywhere at San Simeon, not to mention anywhere else in her widespread body of work in California.

The pool as we know it today is the third design. The first design was in the shape of a cloverleaf and very much smaller than the present pool. Very quickly this apparently proved inadequate for Mr. Hearst soon opted for an enlargement, bringing it up to the size and shape of the inner oval which is today indicated by the dark, Verde Antique marble along the floor of the pool. After this adjustment was made, another alteration became necessary. The series of seven Carrara marble statues, which had been commissioned of Charles Cassou, arrived from Paris. They so dwarfed the existing pool that a further enlargement was called for to bring the entire pool complex into scale. From this second-stage oval shape, the pool was extended to an even larger oval. The square-shaped alcove where Cassou's ''Birth of Venus'' statue is located was added, and the marble colonnades and ancient Roman temple were erected along the edges of the new pool as well. The setting seems so perfect today, yet one wonders whether Mr. Hearst envisioned still further changes and improvements. It would appear to us that a point of relative perfection had finally been attained, but who's to know exactly what his fertile imagination would have conjured up had building gone on at San Simeon beyond 1947?

Along with the cast concrete lamp standards are massive balustrades of the same material. These are done in the classical style and are seen not only at the Neptune Pool but along most of the terraces too. Variations were introduced in the design of the balusters themselves, but, generally speaking, the classical feeling in them is consistent and reminds the visitor constantly of the Mediterranean heritage of San Simeon.

As we have mentioned, six or seven of the original glass globes from Mr. Hearst's time are still intact and in place from the 1920s; these original globes remain in the alcove of the Neptune Pool. Their age is indicated by their lavender coloration, a result of the manganese-bearing glass that was used years ago. This makes for a little gallery of nostalgic, purpled glass in an architectural setting—a collectable which bottle-hunters would no doubt love to have for their own.

The other side of the pool would have had a similar statuary group. The space where they were to be placed, at the top of the wall, is visible today as an empty niche; only the central marble figure is in place, kneeling on her knees, with her hands clasped behind her head. There were to be two flanking figures which were at one time located on the pavement below the niche, awaiting placement in the space above. They have since been moved to the unfinished walkway just below the Grand Entrance steps on the north side of hilltop. The artist for both of the three-piece statuary groups was the same man: Paul Manaut of France.

The sumptuous alcove of the Indoor Swimming Pool is home to "Abundantia," a seventeenth century Italian statue. The cantilevered structure above the alcove is a diving balcony.

The Indoor Swimming Pool as viewed from the diving balcony.

The Indoor Pool; "Abundantia."

In predictable fashion for a man of such wealth and love of luxury, Mr. Hearst saw to it that each of the dressing rooms was provided with its own stall shower, full-length mirror, vanity dressing table — and for the ladies, so legend has it, a full assortment of fine perfumes and cosmetics.

A statuary group of three young women is the only non-classical grouping, either in form or content, near the Neptune Pool, yet they are Parisian-type Moderne or Art Deco nonetheless, and thus classical in spirit. What appears to be a 1920s starlet is sunning herself on top of the wall.

Stairs leading to the next level are bordered by star jasmine, azaleas, and camellias. Twin sets of stairways rise from the pool level above the fountain to a semicircular ring of dressing rooms built into the hill. These form the support for the Neptune Terrace above. The doorway in the center leads to a bank of seventeen dressing rooms. These rooms are not normally shown on tour, but occasionally the door is open and visitors can look in. Bathing apparel was provided by the host so that every one could participate. The solution was a good one because necessary space was provided without further encumbering the garden. The individual dressing rooms each had their own shower facilities.

Above the dressing rooms is the Neptune Terrace surrounded by beautiful trees and shrubs. The planted area between the Neptune Terrace and the pool contains the various

Reproduction of "Apoxyomenos."

View from the back of the diving balcony in the Indoor Pool.

cypresses brought fully grown from Paso Robles and beautifully maintained by the State.

Each year a special tree-crew comes in to trim the Italian cypresses and other large trees on the grounds. It is a remarkable sight to see the trimming of the tall trees which grow closest to the south end of the Neptune Pool. While most of the cypresses, palms, and large oaks can be reached by a hydraulic lift on the back of the crew's truck, the six cypresses near Casa del Sol, can be reached only by rigging up ladders and ropes. It seems that the trees would keel over under the weight of a man hanging on to a ladder toward the top of the tree where it narrows. But the trees are well established, being nearly 100 years old, and the weight does not seem to disturb them. Once the ladder is in place, the crew member given this special assignment dangles to right and left, reaching around and behind the tree with a pair of electric hedge clippers. Below, his crew mates stand by, watching carefully in case assistance is needed. The ladder is roped to the nearby cast concrete balustrades just to be on the safe side. Other workmen on the Castle grounds stop work in order to provide any assistance when these particular trees are getting their trim.

The Villa built by the Roman Emperor Hadrian in Tivoli outside Rome also contains a pool with semicircular ends surrounded by a colonnade and marble statues. Hadrian's Pool was much larger than Mr. Hearst's, but then, he had the gross national product of the Roman Empire behind him, and even Mr. Hearst could not match that.

Of course for all the ingenuity of the Romans and the power enjoyed by an Emperor like Hadrian, such things as electricity to light the colonnades around the pool, coal-oil to warm the water itself, plus such luxuries and comforts as limousines to convey guests up to the hill were either completely unknown during Hadrian's time or existed only in the most primitive ancient-world equivalents. All things considered, Mr. Hearst had things a good deal more to his advantage than old Hadrian did.

Below the Guest Houses, the major terraces include the narrow terrace below Casa del Mar ("A" House) which is not seen on any tour at this writing; the terrace below Casa del Sol ("C" House); the Neptune Pool and Terrace complex; the long terrace below Casa del Monte ("B" House), with the unfinished grand entrance; and finally, the Roman Pool and Tennis Court built around 1930.

The terrace below Casa del Mar ("A" House) is on a steep slope. Casa del Mar was the first structure to be conceived and built as an inexpensive one-story wood bungalow. On the terrace side, however, it appears five stories high. The chief items of interest here are the twin fountains of Italian Mannerist design. In fact, they are replicas of a fountain at the Villa Petraia near Florence.

Poetry in marble; the "Three Graces" — "Brilliance," "Joy," and "Bloom " by Boyer after Antonio Canova.

This fountain is a copy. The famous original, built about 1545, stands near Florence. The structure of the Florence masterpiece was designed by Niccolo Tribolo and Pierino da Vinci, both of whom lived in the first half of the sixteenth century. The fountain supports a statue by Jean Boulogne (1529–1608). This figure represents Venus drying her hair and she has a graceful movement, more in the tradition of seventeenth century Baroque statuary. Boulogne, known as Giovanni da Bologna, or Giambologna, is considered by art critics today to be the most successful follower of Michelangelo.

The fountains below Casa del Mar are duplicates of the Villa Petraia fountains, but the "A" House fountain statues have a distinct 1920s quality and appear unrelated to the Venus figure mentioned above. They portray two nude women who are called "First Rose" and "Fairy Princess."

A similar fountain, seen on Tour One, stands in front of Casa del Sol ("C" House). This fountain consists of a pool at the base rising to a saucer from which water drips into the basin below. At the very top is a bronze statue, a copy of the David by Donatello, which is unfortunately not seen to advantage in this particular location. Behind the fountain, the basin of which is supported by four lions reminiscent of those in the Court of the Lions at the Alhambra in Spain, lies the facade of Casa del Sol ("C" House), with its Spanish loggia, or porch, facing west toward the ocean.

With a pair of field glasses one can examine the artifacts on the west elevation of Casa del Sol ("C" House). Like the other guest houses, Casa del Sol stands on the crest of the hill so that what will appear as a one-story house from above is three to five stories below. A combination of paths, landings, and stairs leads to the doors at the lower level. On the balcony of the loggia in the center between the supporting columns, the visitor can obtain his first glimpses of one of the many Roman sarcophagi which lie at random in the upper garden. The carving on the front is not figurative but geometric. On the lower level, near a pair of curious lions with rings in their mouths, which appear to guard a late sixteenth century Florentine door grille, a bomb exploded at the time that Patricia Hearst was kidnapped and damaged the loggia above. The State has closed the damaged sections for repair and restoration.

The fountain below Casa del Sol is actually two fountains in a combined arrangement, one placed on top of the other for the sake of height and proportion in this setting. A copy of Donatello's "David" crowns the composite fountain. Behind and off to the sides of the assemblage are two marble sculptures by the twentieth century European sculptor, Denys Peuch. One is "Les Lys" (the Lilies), the other "The Roses." Both are in the somewhat sentimental classical style so common in the late nineteenth and early twentieth centuries. Directly behind the fountain is the work of Arthur C. Walker, an American sculptor: "Adam and Eve" in bronze. The west elevation of Casa del Sol (directly above the courtyard just described) presents an interesting combination of elements giving

Most ancient of San Simeon's numerous sculptures are these diorite figures of "Sekhmet" — Egyptian of the Eighteenth and Nineteenth Dynasties.

This statuary group, "The Three Graces," was one of William Randolph Hearst's favorites. The figures represent Brilliance (Aglaia), Joy (Euphrosyne), and Bloom (Thalia).

A front view of "Sekhmet." The head on the right retains its original solar disc.

an agreeable Spanish–Italian design. Some of the features are old and some are from the 1920s. The loggia itself consists of two Spanish columns, a Roman sarcophagus in between the columns, and, before the bomb of 1976 took its toll, a French lantern hung in place from a Spanish-style ceiling. Immediately below the loggia is a grille door leading to the lower floor of the building The grille is Florentine and the flanking window grates in intricate wrought iron are Spanish. Right in front of the doorway squat two Spanish lion sculptures with huge iron rings in their mouths. Down a couple of steps from this porch level, a wrought iron openwork balustrade runs between two concrete supports. This piece of ironwork was done by Ed Trinkeller, one of Julia Morgan's top craftsmen, in response to the Florentine and Spanish work nearby. This one example alone speaks quite admirably for all of the work done by Trinkeller over the years in the building of the Castle.

In the opposite direction, it is the view of the sea sweeping away to the north with the Piedras Blancas Lighthouse in the distance which is compelling. This ever-changing view varies with the weather and the time of day. The terrace is broad despite the slope of the hill. This breadth is made possible by a high wall in which four large palms are incongruously placed. The continual growth of these palms and the fact that their root system has not cracked the wall is a testament to the care they receive from the State and the engineering skill of architect Julia Morgan.

The Casa del Sol Terrace contains two bronze statues near the stairways. The statues were perhaps intended to be the top pieces of two additional Mannerist fountains to be constructed here. The flooring of the terrace seems to support this theory. It has two unfinished sections of the size needed for the base of such fountains. The statues are "Discobolus," a twentieth century copy of the classic discus thrower, and "Winged Victory," a copy of Nike of Brescia. She is an attendant of Athena, the War Goddess. Nike is usually seen as a winged figure carrying an item which is viewed, at times, as a shield, a mirror or a writing tablet. She sometimes wears a crown or garland of honor and success.

Another sculpture near the Casa del Sol Terrace (or "C" Terrace) should be mentioned. This is the marble figure of "Hiawatha," half kneeling, half sitting on a concrete pedestal just south of "C" Terrace and above the hillside where it drops into the brushy canyon. Mr. Hearst's interest in Indians, expressed in part through his fine collection of Navajo blankets and Indian baskets, may have prompted him to have this statue in the gardens. Or maybe he simply thought of it as an attractive piece of outdoor statuary regardless of the subject itself. On the base of "Hiawatha" is this signature and date: J. Mozier, Roma, 1859.

To the east of the Neptune Pool is the North Terrace which contains numerous and varied art objects including, but not limited to, Italian Renaissance carved stone wellheads, a Span-

ish cannon from Cuba, and large Greek terra-cotta storage jars from Southern Italy. The jars, of unknown age, were used to store grains or liquids such as oil and wine. They were partially buried to compensate for the lack of stability in their shape. Those at the Castle are displayed on special stands. Jars from Tuscany, Rome, and Sicily are also on the grounds.

Also on the North Terrace are two stubby mortars — souvenirs, we might say, of the Spanish–American War, with which the name of William Randolph Hearst has always been connected. Each of the mortars bears a bronze plaque on its wooden carriage which states that the pieces were removed from Morro Castle in Havana, Cuba, after the Spanish–American War, 1899. Visitors often remark on seeing the mortars and the nearby cannon, wondering whether they were literally for defense of the Castle. They were never fired during Mr. Hearst's time to our knowledge; they simply made interesting and somewhat fanciful exterior decorations for the grounds of the estate.

Below North Terrace lies the unfinished grand staircase mentioned earlier in this chapter. It is covered with ivy. From here the stairs lead up to an intermediate terrace, then to the Esplanade, and finally to the main terrace and garden in front of the Castle.

Had the Grand Entrance been finished it no doubt would have been one of the most impressive architectural components of the Enchanted Hill. It was never carried past the stage of the pouring of the concrete, but despite its roughness, one can see what it was intended to be. Steps lead up to the North Terrace in a right-hand and left-hand flight, thus conforming to the intentioned symmetry of the San Simeon's architecture. The steps are widely placed, like those of a great palace or public building, as indeed they should be for a building as monumental as La Casa Grande, below which the Grand Entrance lies. Today ivy increasingly covers over the concrete hulk of the steps and walls of the Entrance. Giant rusted reinforcing rods like brown sprouts stick upright out of the steps where cast concrete balustrades of the type seen all over the hill were intended to be installed. Below the surmounting North Terrace is a sheer cliff of concrete probably fifteen feet in height — a descent from the top of the Grand Entrance to the unfinished reflecting pool in between the two great flights of steps. Probably some statues or sculpture of some kind would have been placed in the rectangular pool which sits empty today.

If one were free to wander in the garden, walking around the Esplanade counterclockwise, he or she would be offered the most comprehensive view of the major portion of the site. All the major architectural elements would successively come into view in a short range. La Casa del Monte, "B" House; La Casa del Sol, "C" House; La Casa del Mar, "A" House; and La Casa Grande, could each be successively seen. "Girl with Kid," "The Wrestlers," the late Roman sarcophagus, "Mercury Rest-

A Roman sarcophagus carved in high relief from a solid block of marble. The figures represent the nine Muses and date from the third century A.D..

ing," "Crouching Venus," the "Venus of Cyrene," "Europa and the Bull," the Pan Court, the early Roman sarcophagus beneath the statue of the "Three Graces," the Egyptian group, and finally the statue of Galetea would be visible.

Moving around the Esplanade, large and small scale landscape on the downhill slope provides a screen through which the distant mountains can be seen between Casa del Monte and Casa del Sol and the sea between Casa del Sol and Casa del Mar. After Casa del Mar the dense growth gives way to the South Terrace, slightly lower than the Esplanade. Here the commanding view of the southern coastline is truly spectacular. To the right a large circular wellhead stands close to Casa del Mar. In itself it has no special artistic merit, but it has great historical interest because it was brought from Phoebe's estate in Pleasanton during the 1920s after her death.

Not to be excluded in our view toward the south is what we can see right before us on the other side of the South Terrace, the old wood barracks from the 1920s. The main barracks building was the Switchboard Building in Hearst's time;

now it's the headquarters for the State of California's Historical Monument Operation. As the Switchboard center during Mr. Hearst's time it no doubt had about it the lively atmosphere of the city room of one of Mr. Hearst's large, metropolitan newspapers, but in this instance it was on a rather miniature scale. Nevertheless, it did business twenty-four hours a day. The telephone probably rang continuously, the ticker tape spewed its results without end, the telegraph lines sparked their messages to points on the other side of the globe. The hubbub that must have prevailed through much of the Hearst era is to be no longer. Probably even Mr. Hearst's guests were unaware of how important this building was. While they romped and played, serious business went on behind the scenes almost nonstop until Mr. Hearst's departure from the Enchanted Hill in 1947.

The Main Terrace directly in front of La Casa Grande is surrounded by planting beds with Magnolia grandiflora, Chinese magnolia and Live Oak trees. Other plantings included camellias, azaleas and rhododendrons beneath the large trees. The

fish pond and benches were carved of Italian marble by Mr. Cardini of Lucca, Italy for the Enchanted Hill. The statue in the pool is the nymph, "Galatea on a Dolphin." Galatea was one of the fifty Nereids, daughters of Nerus and Doris. The water of the pool was a favorite drinking spot of Mr. Hearst's dachshunds. After finding one of his favorites, Helen, caught in the pool and unable to get out because of the steep sides, Mr. Hearst had a wooden ladder built and placed in the pool, so that this would not happen again. The ladder is below the front of the statue. A first century Roman tombstone and a carved marble wellhead are across from each other on the Main Terrace.

The Indoor Swimming Pool seems to have had an uncertain fate. One end is buried in the ground and the roof is flat to provide space for the tennis courts. The concrete arches were, no doubt, intended to be faced with stone. In its completed state it could have been similar to, but considerably smaller than the Orangerie at Versailles. (The Orangerie at Versailles is a building partly constructed underground to protect potted citrus trees from freezing in winter.) It acted as a kind of terminus for the northeast end of the garden. The roof is on a level with the Esplanade and the azalea walk while the lower floor opens directly on the rear driveway for no apparent reason. The interior was lavishly decorated with Venetian mosaic of rich blue color laced with gold. Large scale marble statues are placed around the pool in an arbitrary fashion. One is left with the impression that early enthusiasm waned and the enterprise languished for lack of attention. The pool is known as the Roman Pool, but the structure has no counterpart in Roman antiquity. Concrete was used by the Romans but not reinforcing steel, so that a flat structural roof of any span would have been impossible. To be Roman it would have had to be vaulted, but then it could not have been used as a base for the Tennis Courts. The sunny quality of the Neptune Pool is absent so that this one was evidently not popular with the guests.

The interior is now far more interesting than a few years ago. The State has spent a considerable sum of money resurfacing the Tennis Courts which, incidently, has solved a bad

Marble relief entitled ``Nymphs and Satyr'' by the Parisian sculptor S. Muzanne

leakage problem, so that the deteriorated ceiling can now be safely restored. A large skylight between the tennis courts has been opened, allowing light to penetrate the leg of the "T"-shaped pool, making it a sparkling blue grotto.

The main section of the pool is eighty-one feet by thirty-one feet and ten feet in depth. The pool has a flat bottom and the apparent curvature we see is an optical illusion. The leg section of the "T" is a four-foot deep wading pool. The complex took three years to construct, and remains unfinished.

The 205,000 gallons of water reflect gold tile. The tiles were made with gold leaf fused within glass. Original touches are provided by alabaster shades on marble lamp standards around the edge of the pool. A mosaic covered concrete diving platform is between the wading pool and the main section, and is reached by narrow steep staircases on each side. Separate mens' and womens' restrooms and dressing rooms are located on each side of the wading pool. Behind the pool is the heating and filtering system.

The exterior of the Indoor Swimming Pool was not only left unfinished, but on the east side of the structure a nest of reinforcing bars sticks out from the wall in an almost menacing way. Did Mr. Hearst plan to attach something to the existing building at this point? Or did someone simply miscalculate in the course of setting the steel bars for the concrete work and fail to trim off the exposed ends after the forms were removed? The question is impossible to answer without looking over original plans and drawings for this part of the overall building program. And who knows whether the planned-for addition, if one actually had been planned, would have materialized at all? Mr. Hearst may have changed his mind, as he so often did in such matters.

The statue reputed to have been Mr. Hearst's favorite stands directly in front of the entrance to Casa del Mar. The original, "Three Graces" by Antonio Canova, is at the Hermitage in Leningrad. The copy in the Hearst collection is the work of the French sculptor Boyer. The available reference sources list a number of sculptors named Boyer. The information in the possession of the Castle does not identify which Mr. Boyer made this copy. The Graces are Brilliance (Aglaia), Joy (Euphrosyne), and Bloom (Thalia). The Graces are goddesses presiding over the banquet, the dance, and all social enjoyments and elegant arts.

Above the South Terrace along the Esplanade are two statues in a setting that seems to epitomize the entire placement of art objects on the hilltop. The two main figures are the lioness-faced Egyptian goddess, Sekhmet. The carvings are attributed to the Eighteenth Dynasty and could be 3,400 years old. The stone is diorite and is similar in color to the stone of the fountain, but harder. The base of the fountain is made to reflect an Egyptian theme. It is rendered in the Art Deco style of the 1920s. Behind the statue are two curved stairways with Renaissance balustrades and Italian Gothic columns. The risers

One of the several lion motifs. This one stands at the base of the fountain in front of Casa del Sol ("C" House).

This lion figure, with a ring in its mouth, is located on the west side of Casa del Sol.

of the stairs are Spanish-style tile. So we have, in one spot, Egyptian statues on an art deco 1920s base flanked by Italian Renaissance balustrades with Italian Gothic columns and Spanish-style tile risers. The combination is eclectic and quite beautiful.

Although the Roman sarcophagi were mentioned earlier, we might make this additional statement about them. The word sarcophagus literally means flesh-eating stone. Many were created in ancient Rome and were usually made of limestone. The chemical action of the stone caused the bodies placed within them to decompose and vanish, nature's own way of dealing with a problem as old as the human race. While none are famous, all are of great interest to us.

The sarcophagi number nine, including the small one in front of Casa del Sol with a Christian symbol on the front. One of them still retains its cover, which is unusual as they were generally broken by grave robbers hunting for valuables buried in the coffin. The covered sarcophagus has an inscription which translates, "To the very great Insteau who lived twenty years and nine months."

We can now return to the terrace in front of the facade of La Casa Grande, which we will explore in the next chapter.

A fountain detail from the Court of the Lions in Granada, Spain.

"Mars and Cupid" by Prof. Umberto Marcellini, Naples, 1929.

Preliminary drawing by Julia Morgan for the west facade of La Casa Grande.

C H A P T E R 6

THE ARCHITECTURE

A frequent legitimate question asked by visitors is, "But Mr. Winslow, isn't it [the Castle and the collection] a hodge podge?" With this question the visitor unwittingly penetrates the depth of the idea behind the Castle design and the collection it was intended to house. Indeed, it would appear from what W.A. Swanberg writes in *Citizen Hearst* (p. 425 of the paperback edition), that Mr. Hearst "was fond of paraphrasing Emerson by saying, 'Consistency is the hobgoblin of little minds.'" By this measure Mr. Hearst certainly had a large and encompassing mind. Eclecticism, perhaps, is a more accurate description of the Castle and its contents than hodge podge.

Art historians frequently divide historical movements into manageable periods called early, high, and late, as in the Gothic periods. The kind of eclecticism we find in Mr. Hearst's collecting habits would certainly fall into the category of the "high period of eclecticism." Since the Castle was built during the 1920s and 1930s, its art collection derives from potential sources of that period.

Mr. Hearst's eclecticism follows that practiced by the Roman Emperor Hadrian when he erected his villa at Tivoli outside Rome. In fact, many of the same elements are found at Hearst Castle, such as the outdoor pool with curved ends, semicircular colonnade at the end, and classical sculpture throughout. Beyond this the comparison no longer works: Hadrian had only the styles of Greece and Rome to draw on, whereas Mr. Hearst had a much wider palate. Hadrian's work was larger for

Neuschwanstein, one of the nineteenth century dream castles of Ludwig II of Bavaria Germany.

he had the Roman Empire behind him, whereas Hearst had a comparably modest albeit substantial corporation. However, it is probably true that Mr. Hearst had more land in his own name than Hadrian. Apart from these statistical differences, and allowing for the gap in time between the Roman Empire and twentieth century America, their fundamental intentions remain the same. Both men were collectors of architecture on a worldwide basis. Because of size, architecture is difficult to relocate, so the next best thing is to try to recreate it. Hadrian generally imitated other works at his Villa. Hearst imitated too, but, where possible, he imported the genuine article.

Eclecticism beginning with Hadrian enjoys sporadic and isolated renewal from time to time in history, and comes to its height in the nineteenth century, at which time antiquities from China, India, and the Far East broaden the collector's potential. Pure revival, of course, is quite different from eclecticism. In the nineteenth century when the simple medieval county fair became a worldwide phenomenon on an architectural scale, eclecticism became popular. This movement reached a climax in the Great White City — the Chicago Exposition of 1893, at once extolled and derided. This fair was followed by similar, if less spectacular, fairs in Paris in 1900; St. Louis in 1904; Omaha; and ultimately the Panama Pacific Exposition in San Francisco in 1915, which immediately preceded the building of the Hearst Castle.

Among the romantically conceived world's fairs of the turn of the century period, the 1915 Panama–California Exposition in San Diego would seem to have had a significant bearing on what was designed and built for William Randolph Hearst at San Simeon just a few years later. If not a matter of direct influence, it was at least a matter of the architects and designers of the San Diego fair holding ideals quite similar to those so frequently expressed by Mr. Hearst. San Diego marked the turning point for what had been slowing down as an architectural movement: California's Mission Revival style of the 1890s and first five or ten years of this century. With the new work appearing on the exposition grounds at Balboa Park under the direction of the famous Bertram Grosvenor Goodhue and his chief assistant, Carleton Winslow, Sr., the Mission look was given a much-needed shot in the arm. From the time of San Diego on into the 1930s when the Depression finally dissolved the movement, the earlier and very numerous California buildings in the Mission Style — oftentimes heavy, clumsy, and devoid of grace — were widely superseded by a more exotic, fanciful, and, above all, sophisticated romanticism of Spanish Colonial inspiration — hence the new term Spanish Colonial Revival to take up where Mission was leaving off. Instead of overly massive, rounded arches — such as can be seen on surviving Mission Revival railroad depots in Santa Barbara and

La Casa Grande and main garden area in a rarely photographed view from one of the tower rooms in La Casa del Sol.

The Neptune Pool; looking through the north colonnade to the ancient Roman temple and south colonnade beyond.

Old world inspiration for new world builders — the Acropolis in Athens, Greece.

other California towns — civic, commercial, and especially private buildings began to assume striking personalities and guises more reminiscent of Mexico City, Guadalajara, Lima, or even a Spanish city in the old country itself. Tile-work increased in importance as did wrought iron work for window grilles, doors, and gates. Intricate stucco and cast concrete decoration proliferated — in short, the romantic tendencies seemingly inherent in California life and architecture moved into a more mature stage of expression. The lavish taste of William Randolph Hearst was naturally quite favorably disposed to this enhancement of the Latin idiom only vaguely revealed in the older Mission Style. The California Building on the San Diego fairgrounds showed how detailed and complex Spanish Colonial ornamentation could get. The term Churrigueresque came into use in this part of the world — a reference to the ultra-elaborate decoration and ornament of the Baroque architect Jose Churriguera. Many consider Goodhue's California Tower in Balboa Park the gem of Spanish Colonial Revival design; many have since come to notice that the towers of La Casa Grande at San Simeon bear a striking resemblance to the 1915 work in San Diego. Very likely Mr. Hearst consciously or unconsciously availed himself of a fresh and vibrant model that was near — and recent — at hand. And Julia Morgan very likely found the San Diego Exposition a viable point of departure for the new job underway at San Simeon too.

The nineteenth century also saw other adventures in eclecticism, more nearly comparable to Hearst Castle, such as the castles of Neuschwanstein and Linderhoff by Ludwig II of Bavaria. They are all called castles, but none serve any military purpose whatsoever.

In the United States the eclectic spirit of the nineteenth and early twentieth centuries gave rise to numerous mansions and private grand residences in architectural derivations and mixtures of widely varying type. These earlier efforts are the precursors, the immediate ancestors of Hearst Castle, the Castle being the last of the great episodes of its kind — and certainly the most considerable — on the part of any wealthy American. At the forefront of the pre–San Simeon highlights in American dream-house architecture is Biltmore in Asheville, North Carolina, the monumental country seat of George Washington Vanderbilt. Other Vanderbilt mansions along with chateau-like, castle-like, and palace-like structures erected by various ultra-rich families still exist in the summer resort of Newport, Rhode Island. Pre-eminent among these are the "Breakers" and "Marble House." In Florida, the efforts of James Deering; in Miami, and in Sarasota, the Ringlings are memorable. These and many other American palaces and castles, whether they still stand today or have long since been razed, have in common a borrowing from established architectural traditions, a sense about them of monumentality and grandeur, a certain willingness to

La Casa del Monte's sun-drenched south court. "Mercury Resting" at left.

toy and play with historical precedent for the sake of making a latter-day version more lively and interesting. Without exception, they all have in common a predating of the building of San Simeon, oftentimes by a matter of decades and not just years. Thus a rich legacy of eclecticism and architectural romanticism stood behind William Randolph Hearst when it came time for him to build *his* dream house.

By the time Mr. Hearst started building his castle, a sober Europe was recovering from World War I and an angry America embarked on a final roaring fling before the Depression of the 1930s which closed an era begun in the early years of the nineteenth century. Mr. Hearst got a late start and continued his building program long after a world, weary of architectural opulence, had turned, in part, to the more astringent forms of modern architecture. By the time the construction of the Castle was in full force in the 1930s, the Castle (and other buildings like it) had come to represent everything distasteful in the Victorian Age without, itself, having Victorian features. Hearst Castle was destined to be consigned to temporary oblivion; Julia Morgan's abhorrence of publicity mattered little, because the undertaking was far removed from the new direction architecture was taking. One of the authors, a product of architectural education in the late 1930s, visited the Castle in 1958, shortly after it was opened to the public, and decided that the building represented everything he had been taught to mis-

A glimpse of La Casa Grande's Main Vestibule through the gilded doorway of the Assembly Room.

The Doge's Palace in Venice, Italy.

A symphony of stone arches and windows on the rear elevation of La Casa Grande.

trust — it was the perfect example of the evil forces of revivalism and eclecticism at work. The recent highly publicized ''death'' of modern architecture now permits us to confront such works in a less prejudiced, objective frame of mind.

We can now turn to examine the architectural elements of the Castle. The first consideration is the siting — the building's relationship to its environment. John Beach of San Francisco, a keen observer of the architectural scene, has said, ''It is all very well, but I think he overbuilt the neighborhood.'' We don't agree. If you are going to hold your own with the Pacific Ocean, the blue sky of the Central Coast, and the entire range of the Santa Lucia Mountains, anything but the boldest statement would be lost. The actual location of the building was probably not specifically chosen by either Miss Morgan or her client. It had proven to be a worthy camp site in the late nineteenth century when George Hearst had purchased the land and established it as his working ranch.

One approaches the Castle over a winding road which follows approximately the old trail. The Castle is clearly visible from below, crossing the coastal shelf, but disappears from view when one reaches the lower foothills. Then its towers reappear and disappear again as the visitor moves in and out of the ridges and ravines, and under and behind the California Live Oaks. At the top of the ridge the Castle vanishes in the pines planted by Mr. Hearst and is not fully seen again until

One of the New Wing's long hallways. Ceiling and lanterns are Spanish.

A Venetian loggia reminiscent of the Doge's Palace facade decorates the exterior of the Doge's Suite in La Casa Grande.

one stands directly in front. The experience of approaching the Parthenon at the Acropolis in Athens is similar. The Parthenon is fully visible from the neighboring hill, disappears as one starts up the slope, and remains invisible until the visitor moves through the gateway or propylea when, at last, it is fully in view. In the case of Hearst Castle, this may not have been intentional, but it is the result.

Earth moving equipment — except for mules, scrape boards, and steam shovels — was not available to builders in the early 1920s, and the idea of shearing off the top of a mountain had not become the practice as it is today. Julia Morgan was required to fit the building to the site, which accounts for the multi-level changes in the garden. In a very real sense the building completes the crest of the hill, rather than competing with it. So perfectly does the building fit the site that a better solution appears impossible to imagine. If for no other reason than its superb siting, the Castle deserves a high mark.

Let us turn our attention to the individual buildings. Apart from the temporary service structures put up by the State — a rather nice ad hoc touch is the adapted mobile home used as a guide trailer — and various support structures, the buildings are five in number:

Three guest houses: Casa del Mar (''A'' House), Casa del Monte (''B'' House), and Casa del Sol (''C'' House); A great house: La Casa Grande; A gymnasium unit with swimming pool and support facilities inside and tennis courts on the roof, the indoor or Roman Pool. We can dispense with the gymnasium as such by saying that it is no larger than most junior high school gyms, but falls far short of the excellent women's gym which Julia Morgan designed with Bernard Maybeck at the University of California at Berkeley. A series of round arches cast in cement indicates an attempt to deal with the aesthetic problem, but the necessity of rooftop tennis courts rendered hopeless any attempt to make the building conform to a Spanish or Italian model. It is curious that so much attention would have been devoted to the mosaic of the interior and so little to the exterior. One wonders, on examining the exterior with wires and reinforcing bars extending through the concrete, what the finishing touches might have been.

The guest houses are quite different in detail and size, but all are remarkably similar in style. They come closer to being Italian and Spanish than anything else. It must be remembered that examples of pure architectural styling are rare if nonexistent on the hill. A case in point is the Casa del Sol (''C'' House); it reflects a Spanish influence with decided Italian overtones. They were all designed in a typical Julia Morgan style, using formal symmetry. The flat soffits under the eaves are decorated with molded plaster figures, and the formal organization of the windows shows a kinship with the Italian country house. The Spanish were a little less formal in their smaller scale domestic work. The Italian influence is further confirmed by the use of the dual Mannerist fountains below the Casa del

At the north end of the walnut-paneled Library Lobby can be seen a similarly decorated Otis elevator that is still in use today.

Gilded plaster caryatids and damask-lined walls lend an air of whimsy and elegance to the Theater.

Two fifteenth century Spanish "wildmen" guard the iron entry gates of La Casa Grande. The equestrian figure and virgin and child group above the door are likewise from the Hearst sculpture collection. Carved and cast stone work of the 1920s completes the illusion of A Northern Spanish cathedral.

Mar ("A" House) which we discussed in the previous chapter and which are very similar to those at the Villa Petraia near Florence. There is a similar fountain in front of the Casa del Sol ("C" House). This fountain is crowned by a copy of "David".

The first building to be built on the hilltop was the Casa del Mar ("A" House). Construction was begun in 1919 and Mr. Hearst occupied the building in 1921. This is perhaps the most interesting of the three guest houses for several reasons. It is the largest, close to five stories in height in the back. The steep slope of the hill necessitated construction in such a way. From the front it appears to be a single story bungalow, but in fact is the only guest house with an interior staircase. (Casa del Sol has two *small* series of steps leading to its towers.)

Access to the Casa del Mar is made from an entry courtyard, through a single doorway into the vestibule area. Within the vestibule are two narrow staircases which descend to the lower level. On the top floor are four bedrooms, two bathrooms, and a living room which projects to the rear of the building.

The lower level consists of two bedrooms, two bathrooms, and a sitting room. When the Hearst family was still utilizing this guest house, the east lower bedroom and a large walk-in closet were converted into a pantry and kitchen. The sitting room area was then used as a dining room. In all, there are fourteen rooms in Casa del Mar, including the bathrooms.

Restoration and rehabilitation on the hilltop is a never ending project. On Casa del Mar alone the State has recently finished an extensive restoration project of the highly decorative and unique molded plaster soffits which had deteriorated. Walter Steilberg, who worked for Julia Morgan, said that there had been limited rehabilitation work done on the house even when Mr. Hearst lived in it. There had previously been a seepage problem in the lower level due to a spring near the house. That has been repaired.

The repair of cast concrete decorative work on Casa del Mar was done in the early 1970s and took over one year to complete. Each section of cast work had to be removed so that it could be exactly duplicated in a process very similar to the one used on the hill in the Twenties. The area back of the old fire station by the Indoor Swimming Pool has been set up as a mold shop where cast work both in concrete and in plaster of Paris can be done on an extensive scale. At this writing, the cast concrete work on Casa del Sol is undergoing the same kind of facelifting that was performed on Casa del Mar a few years ago. The smallest of the Guest Houses, Casa del Monte, is slated to have its cast concrete decoration redone in the near future. For a two year period the facade of La Casa Grande itself was almost completely covered with scaffolding while repairs of this same type were made. Ultimately there will come a day when every bit of cast work on the exteriors of the buildings will have been duplicated and replaced through the efforts of a modern-day staff of skilled craftsmen.

One of numerous prototypes in European architecture for the design of La Casa Grande's facade (Villa d'Este, Italy).

A Spanish prototype — San Gregorio.

Spanish Gothic "wildman" at the front door of La Casa Grande.

The other half of the entryway duo.

Fortunately, it is easier to blend brand new cast concrete or plaster work with remaining old sections than it is to repair woodwork or ironwork and to have the results match any earlier parts left nearby.

Casa del Monte ("B" House) is the smallest of the Guest Houses. It was constructed in 1920 and consists of ten rooms all on a single level. On tour, visitors enter from a sheltered courtyard which contains a statue known as the "Crouching Venus," an exact copy of the original found in the Vatican, then through one of the two sets of double doors, and into the lobby or vestibule.

The tour then proceeds through the first bedroom, two bathrooms, the second bedroom, the twenty-nine by eighteen foot sitting room, the third bedroom, two additional bathrooms and the fourth bedroom. Here one observes the formal symmetry of the house. One side is a mirror image of the other. The mirror image theme carries over to ceilings in bedrooms two and three. The ceilings, which are duplicates, are known as "the twenty-four faces of the hours of the day." Although the faces on each ceiling are all unique and have highly individual expression, the ceiling is repeated in the two rooms.

Perhaps this is a good point to note that the ceilings in all the guest houses were molded on the hilltop by Mr. Vanderloo and his son, from designs by Julia Morgan. Some of the ceilings

A pair of "wildmen" at San Gregorio, Spain.

are painted to look like wood, while others are polychromed, or painted and gold-leafed.

La Casa Grande has its share of molded plaster ceilings also. Scattered through the 100 room mansion are ceiling sections sometimes finished in gold leaf and polychrome *a la* guest houses, and in other cases finished in clever imitation of wood carving, complete with a simulation of knot holes, grain patterns, and marks from the carver's tools. Some claim that even a few antique-looking columns and doors are made of plaster of Paris; it is so difficult to tell where this has been done that we are unable to confirm this theory. A fascinating possibility however.

In the Casa del Monte there are two unusual beds. In the third bedroom is one of the few antique English articles to be found on the hilltop. The bed has a seventeenth century canopied, carved wooden frame. (It must be noted that whether the bed is English or Spanish can be disputed.) In the second bedroom one finds a Northern Italian Lombardic seventeenth century bed made of carved walnut. The headboard is carved to simulate fringed drapery, surrounding a coat of arms of three fish surmounted by a coronet and a bishop's hat. The bed is known as ''Cardinal Richelieu's bed,'' although it was probably not used by him. Over the bed hangs a Flemish armorial tapestry of a seventeenth century cardinal archbishop.

The Casa del Sol (''C'' House) was built in 1921 and is also situated on the hillside. The house has three levels which are divided into eight bedrooms, eight bathrooms, two sitting rooms, and numerous closets and lobby areas.

The main level is seen on tour and the entrance is made through the first bedroom. Before entering, take a good look at the old red Verona marble Byzantine lions near the courtyard and the marvelous iron doors. It is said that Mr. Trinkeller fashioned the faces on the doors after himself and various craftsmen. The workmanship exemplifies the quality of all of the building and crafting which went into Mr. Hearst's concrete dream.

Lack of space makes it impossible to describe it all, but there are several works of art not to miss in the Casa del Sol. In the first bedroom, attention should be given to a painting of ''Madonna and Child'' by Giovanni Salvi (1605–1685) and the lovely thirteenth century dark blue pitcher from Sultanabad, Persia, directly below. Through the rest of the bedrooms in ''C'' House there are a number of beautiful Persian vases and pitchers from the twelfth, thirteenth, and fourteenth centuries. In the fourth bedroom is a bas-relief polychrome glazed group entitled ''Nativity Scene,'' which was fired in Caffagiolo in the fifteenth century.

The second bedroom contains a very fine gilded four-post bed. This is of a type that only the most richly appointed palace could have boasted centuries ago. A couple of extremely fine silk rugs from Persia are used as wall hangings in this same room. Next on the tour through this building is the Sitting

Fifteenth and sixteenth century limestone carvings join with modern stonework in one of Julia Morgan's more complex designs.

Room, which looks very convincingly like the interior of some Spanish grandee's home during the days of Philip II. The walls of red velvet shine with their ''cloth of gold'' applique; along the walls stand Spanish writing desks known as varguenos Casa del Sol's other rooms have their share of art treasures too, which will be described in greater detail in the chapter on The Collection.

While the three guest houses are different in detail and size they have one common characteristic. During the time they were used as guest houses by Mr. Hearst, there were no eating or cooking facilities in them. They served the same function as did the small tents when the hilltop was a campsite. Granted, the guest houses are more opulent and probably more comfortable, but they still acted as satellites to the main tent, La Casa Grande.

The evolution of the guest houses from their wood bungalow beginnings to the final form has already been examined in Chapter III.

We can now turn our attention to La Casa Grande, which is not only large, but complex. At the outset we are confronted with the fact that the front seems reasonably well integrated and finished, while the back is not only unfinished, but delightfully unresolved. It is a sort of concrete easel into which is inserted a vast array of assorted antique stone windows and window frames. Their age is accentuated by their placement in

Bust of St. Peter — Spanish of the sixteenth century.

St. Paul faces the doorway of La Casa Grande from the opposite side of the facade.

an otherwise unadorned concrete wall. In some ways the rear elevation is more interesting than the front. The combination of imported styles with locally built elements is confusing to the architectural historian, if not to anyone else. The dramatic center piece of the rear facade is the stone frame in the center of the second level which opens into the Doge's Suite. The frame consists of four arches and balustrades very similar to those found in the Doge's Palace in Venice, Italy which were designed by Giovanni and Bartholomew Buon, in the early part of the 1400s or the palace of the Ca d'Oro designed by the same architects between 1424 and 1436 for one of the merchant princes of Venice. Most of the other frames in the rear facades and on the flanks of the wings are Gothic in design, some Venetian.

The unfinished rear court as it stands today represents an unresolved architectural situation. The original design produced by Julia Morgan did not contemplate the high four-story wings which compete rather disastrously with the central wing. At first nothing beyond the East Room or Morning Room was contemplated. This one-story section containing the Billiard Room on the north and the Kitchen on the south was added. Then rooms on the first floor were inserted. The servants' wing on the south and the Theater on the north were planned, gradually growing in height as the demand for yet more space continued. This imbalance must have been dis-

turbing to an architect of Julia Morgan's training and experience, but by now, the job was probably out from under her direct control.

> Mr. William Randolph Hearst,
> Ambassador Hotel,
> Los Angeles, California.
>
> Dear Mr. Hearst:
>   To add the studio on the north wing would be virtually the addition of a third story. Would it not unbalance the Patio? A third story on the south also would bring the roof line so high the eaves would be practically on a line with those of the Main Building.
>   Could the studio be housed in the Chinese Hill group, or possibly in the Tennis Court development?
>   Yours very truly,
>   Julia Morgan

From the west facade none of this is at all apparent. In fact, the route of the tour does not reveal the basic symmetry of the entire complex. Here we are confronted by the most bewildering aspect of the entire enterprise: twin towers soaring into the air, the very hallmark, not of any known Castle or country villa, but of a monastery or cathedral. However, the central portal, while impressive, is more in a residential scale. The curious array of balconies, gable ends, windows and doors on the upper level would fragment the facade if it were not for the dominating effect of the towers.

A Spanish design with pronounced Oriental overtones is found in the exotic teakwood gable on the third floor of La Casa Grande. The San Francisco woodcarver Julio Suppo executed this and similar cornice work for the side and rear elevations of the building.

Detail of one of the grotesque brackets in Suppo's gable.

The main facade is certainly the most arresting element in the complex of buildings. The design obviously evolved over a period of time. The "revised" drawing is similar but not identical with the building as it exists today. The windows flanking the main door were not installed because they would have interfered with the installation of the choir stalls on the interior. The towers are quite different from the final solution and the "extra" gable necessitated by the addition of the Celestial Suite does not appear.

On the other hand, the main gable as shown in the drawing is similar to what was installed. The teakwood gable was carved by J. Suppo, an outstanding woodcarver, was contemplated for use here during the initial planning along with the seventeenth century Venetian weather vanes.

The facade is cast in concrete and faced with stone, only a small part of the facade was imported and listed in the "Built-In Inventory" at the Castle. The wrought iron grill at the main entrance is from Spain, but the beautiful fan grill above was fashioned by Ed Trinkeller, who did much of the iron work for Mr. Hearst from designs by Julia Morgan.

Flanking the doorway are two lifesize figures at the jambs. These fifteenth century Spanish figures are unclad but are covered with hair. They each hold shields. They are "wild men," guardians of the entrance, who come from a mysterious tradition with pagan origins in the Early Middle Ages. They serve

Mouldings, balustrades and other architectural details in cast stone — all San Simeon—made in the 1920s.

Gothic-style corner doorway in 1920s cast stone.

The imposing front doorway of La Casa Grande.

the same function as do the lions on Assyrian Palaces, Hittite cities, and Mycenaen citadels. Such guardians are also used decoratively in connection with coats of arms. Similar hairy men guard the entrance to the Colegio de San Gregorio at Valludolid in Spain where the entire facade turns out to be a gigantic representation of the arms of Castille.

Above the door is an equestrian figure of the "Duke of Burgundy Going Hunting" surmounted by a small niche containing a figure of St. Mary with infant Jesus, presumably of thirteenth century Spanish Gothic origin. Reliefs, in the form of carved limestone busts, flanking the main entrance represent St. Peter and St. Paul holding keys and sword respectively. They are late Spanish Gothic, perhaps sixteenth century.

Most accounts of the Castle repeat the story that the towers were inspired by the cathedral of Ronda in Spain. There certainly exists a church in the small town of Ronda that has a rather plain tower square at the base and octagonal above. If this is the inspiration, the connection is very remote. Guide books of the early twentieth century do not indicate that Ronda was ever a cathedral town.

Completing the religious allusion are the bells in the tower which were ordered from Tournai, Belguim where they were cast by Marcel Michaels. Each tower contains a set of eighteen bells which were played from a keyboard adjacent to the Billiard Room.

All other decorative work, including the lintels on either side of the main portal, the horseman frieze on the first balcony in front of the Library, the wrought iron work on the balcony above, and the cast stone and tile decoration on the towers was designed by Julia Morgan and built in California, if not right on the Hill.

The cathedral appearance of the facade suggests that on entering the building a great church nave, or nave-like hall, stretching out in front of the viewer, would be encountered. It is therefore a real shock to find the opposite, a great hall stretching laterally under the towers. Besides being totally unexpected, a perceptive civil engineer or achitect may begin to wonder, while standing in the Assembly Room, what happened to the towers. If he is cognizant of the fact that each tower is made of heavy solid concrete, that each tower contains sets of heavy bells, that each tower holds a 2,500 gallon water storage tank for the entire complex, and further, that the towers seem to slant mysteriously over the fragile wood ceiling, he may become sufficiently apprehensive and choose to escape the building site. This does not occur to most people and the structure of the room is taken for granted. Yet it is so vast, roughly eighty-three feet by thirty-one feet, that the proportions approach those of a dirigible hangar.

Two other elements will strike an architect on entering. First, in this huge room there are only two windows, one at each end, placed so low that they seem to have slipped down to the floor. The choir stalls prevent them from being down too

low and the tapestries prevent them from being up too high. We must remember that the entire room was designed around specific art objects.

The second element which is important to an understanding of the Castle is the lack of stairways. Although medieval architecture was not famous for monumental stairways, since cathedrals were essentially one-story buildings, one might have imagined the dramatic elements of the Baroque staircase found at the Bishop Palace at Wurtzburg or Bruchsal in Germany. One might expect Mr. Hearst to greet his friends from above in regal fashion. Hearst in fact usually made his appearance from a secret panel built into one of the choir stalls.

The two different sets of choir stalls are Italian walnut and are used as paneling around the lower half of the Assembly Room. The choir stalls have carved panels with armrests. Most have their original seats. Some of the carvings are sculptured relief faces and masks. The wood ceiling of the assembly room is greatly restored. It was originally constructed for the sixteenth century Palazzo Martinengo in Brescia, Italy. The massive room is a veritable storehouse of treasures. The size and complexity of it have the effect of overpowering the visitor. On tour, one loses the perspective of the room's utility. A quick look around and a vivid imagination will easily conjure up notable and varied guests playing the piano, listening to the radio, conversing with a friend or simply enjoying a game of Monopoly, while waiting for the host to appear.

The fireplace, with its two torsoed figures each holding a coat of arms, and "The Great Barney Mantel from the Chateau des Jours" are placed centrally like the high altar in a cathedral. A pair of secret panels on either side open to provide access to the rooms exactly opposite, the Refectory or Dining Room. The Refectory is the antithesis of the Assembly Room in both style and layout.

It is Gothic in feeling, rather than Renaissance. Upon entering one looks the length of the room as in a church nave. The windows are high near the ceiling, as opposed to low near the floor as in the Assembly Room. The room also appears to be sealed off from the next major room by a gold plated wrought iron grill.

The sixty-seven by twenty-eight foot Dining Room has a most unusual wood ceiling, possibly from central Italy. It contains figures of saints, such as St. Petronius, patron saint of the city of Bologna in Northern Italy. Just below the wood ceiling hang banners from Siena suspended perpendicularly to the wall in an effective manner. The banners in the Henry VIII Chapel of Westminster Abbey in London produce a similar effect. Of all the rooms in La Casa Grande, this is the most pure in style and the least eclectic. The inspiration is nearly all Gothic.

On entering and seeing the silver items and wooden tables, and observing the general feel of the rooms, the visitor should glance back at the wall through which he has entered. The

A study of contrasting window treatment in the New Wing; simple squares against lacy curved frames.

Another fine window treatment on the east elevation of La Casa Grande.

French Gothic fireplace has been extended horizontally. Set in the concrete extensions are Spanish medallions from the sixteenth century representing Visigothic Kings. The wall, which is a prime example of the visual images created by Gothic architecture, is actually twenty-eight feet wide by twenty-seven feet high. The Gothic arches over the doors and over the fireplace, along with the cement panels, create the illusion of a tall narrow wall.

The next room the visitor enters is the Morning Room. While not particularly important architecturally, it has some special features. After passing through the gold plated iron grill, the visitor passes under an easily unnoticed but extremely beautiful arch. It is made of red Pyrénées marble from the Cathedral of Urgel, and it is one of the many architecturally fine components which Mr. Hearst collected. It appears to be Romanesque on the sides and Gothic on the top. Miss Morgan utilized such pieces with a great sensitivity and a definitive artistic eye.

Across the room from the entry is a vestibule which leads to the back patio. The visitor, though not entering the vestibule, should glance in and note the late Roman mosaic floor, the ceiling, one of seven from the Castle of Benies, Spain, and the two Spanish Renaissance brass braziers which were originally used as portable room heaters.

Before we go on to the technicalities of construction, there

are two suites of rooms which are seen on tours and which need to be examined for their architectural features. Both suites appear on the same tour, as of now, and if your interest lies in Miss Morgan's delightful use of space, try not to miss the Lower South Duplex and the Celestial Suite.

The Lower South Duplex is a suite of rooms consisting of an upper balconied bedroom cantilievered over a sitting room. The bathroom and entry hall are also on the lower level. Entrance was gained on each level by a door to the halls. There is a charming small spiral staircase which connects the two main rooms. The rope handrail leads to a balustrade.

The entire duplex is dominated by the ceiling, which combines painted canvas panels, and four pair of armorial tondi all joined together. The ceiling will be examined later in detail.

The Celestial Suite is located on the fourth floor of La Casa Grande. The two mirror image bedrooms and the sitting room that connects them are all on the same level, and are located within the towers. The two bathrooms for the suite are located on a lower level under the deck which projects from the sitting room. The one story about the concept of the Celestial Suite is that, while visiting Mr. Hearst during the construction of the Castle, Arthur Brisbane is reported to have said how nice it would be to have a room up in the stars. Mr. Hearst followed his friend's fantasy, and ''installed the room,'' so to speak, sometime in the mid-1930s.

The exposed brickwork surrounding this window is a fine example of Mr. Hearst's penchant for incorporating architectural objects into La Casa Grande.

Note the finely carved detail in this window on the exterior of the Billiard Room, La Casa Grande.

Entrance to each bedroom is gained through two archways. Each is supported by rounded columns with composite capitals on elongated rectangular bases. The entire entryway is polychromed and gold-leafed in a floral motif which is enriched by birds, figures and leaves. The rooms themselves are octagonal in shape, with the entryway forming one side of the octagon.

The walls of each bedroom are bas-relief panels with animal figures broken on three sides and small arched doors which lead to triangular decks. Visitors do not have access to these platforms. While such balconies afford the highest and most unobstructed views from the Castle, they are quite small, perhaps accommodating no more than one person at a time. Lighted through grilles, which are covered with transluscent glass, the rooms have no windows in the modern sense. This was done in order to maintain the solid appearance of the towers from the outside. We see this as a basic design conflict where interior function—as in a bedroom, for example—is opposed to exterior form—as might be the case with a church tower. Even in Mr. Hearst's day, these tiny balconies were not always accessible. At the time of his visit, Ludwig Bemelmans recalls that shirt-cardboards were hung on the doors requesting the guests not to go out onto the balconies. The wall coverings are finished with gold silk drapes lined with linen. It has been told to us that, on a night with a full moon, the light shining through the bas-relief makes star patterns around the room.

The Celestial Suite sitting room has an interesting ceiling of deep wooden coffers with plaster trim, painted and gilded. The focal point of the room is the fireplace with its twelfth century French inscription. The inscription, in English, reads, "In this house where heaven and earth shine brightly, live Rafridus, his wife Ada, and the rectors." The stone mason who did the inscription ran out of space while carving, and the last part of the inscription is cramped and runs over, turning the corner and partially printed down the front. The firebox is surrounded by eight fifteenth century tiles from Spain.

In this room the visitor should take the time to glance at the paintings, two works by the late nineteenth century French painter Jean Leon Gerome, "Bonaparte at Cairo" and "Napoleon and the Sphinx," and "Flight into Egypt" by Luc Olivier Merson, a contemporary of Gerome's. Directly opposite the fireplace is a short flight of stone steps. By climbing these steps and looking out past the deck, the visitor can see the Pacific Ocean from one of the highest points on the Enchanted Hill. Access onto the deck is prohibited since it lacks a balustrade. Adding such a rail would severely detract from Julia Morgan's design of the facade.

We now turn our attention to the technical details of construction of the Castle. Cast in-place reinforced concrete was used for all the walls, both interior and exterior (with a spare use of wood-frame partition work). In addition, the floor itself

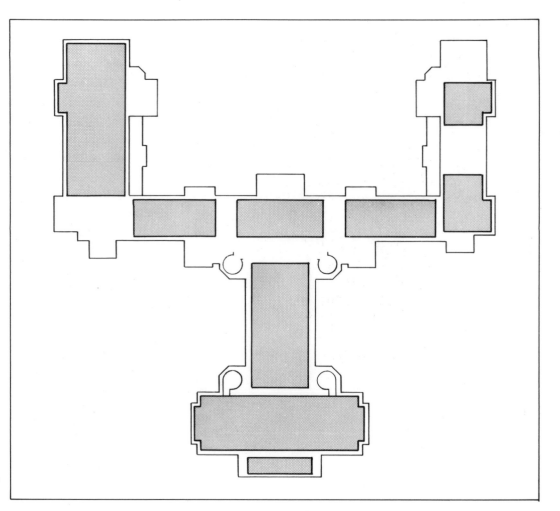

Main Floor diagram of
La Casa Grande.

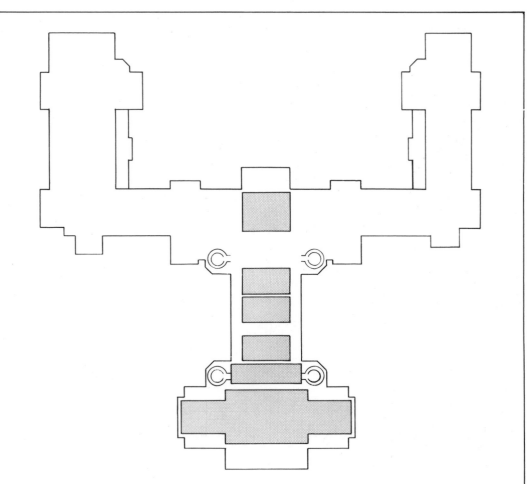

Second Floor diagram.

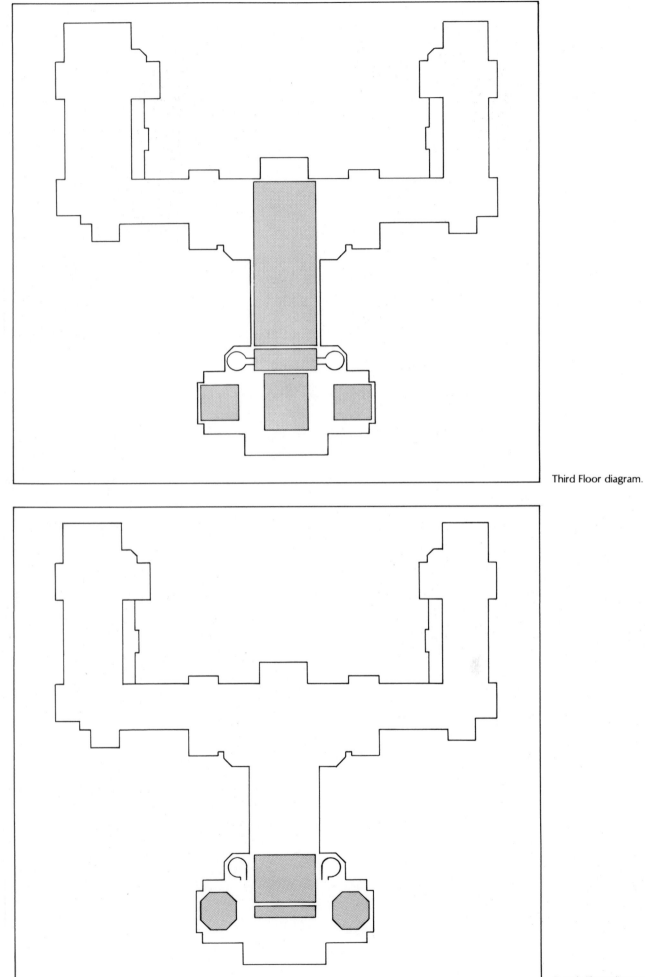

Third Floor diagram.

Fourth Floor diagram.

The Assembly Room as it looked sometime in the 1930s. The guests gathered here to await Mr. Hearst and the call to dinner.

and its supporting structures were made of concrete. Most of the rooms have wood ceilings or plaster ceilings painted to look like wood as in the guest houses. The only room in the Castle where the internal structure is visible to the tourist is in the kitchen where the concrete slabs and trusses are exposed. The servants' quarters above the kitchen are unfinished and structure is visible there, but the tours do not pass through this area. The rooms in the basement, including the abandoned Bowling Alley now used as a restoration workshop, also have exposed concrete ceilings.

The interiors of both stair towers are exposed concrete and there is evidence of unfinished alteration work where sections of the wall have been cut with a jackhammer. Raw concrete appears at the top of the stair towers. Adela Rogers St. Johns said in an interview with the authors that the condition of the stairs was even worse when the Castle was in use. She remembered stumbling as she came down. Emerging at the bottom she encountered Mr. Hearst and Miss Morgan engaged in planning a new section and she suggested rather pointedly that they finish one part before moving on. Her words were not heeded.

Eventually, the concrete would have been entirely covered. At the time the Castle was built, the aesthetic qualities of concrete were not appreciated. In fact reinforced concrete was unknown fifty years prior to the time the Castle was built and it did not come into general use much before 1900. In our time we have seen wider use of exposed concrete in some of our public buildings and in our freeways and have some appreciation of its aesthetic potential.

Reinforced concrete has a structural advantage in that it could be brought onto the site in the form of cement and steel in light bars. The bulk of the concrete, the water, the sand, and the gravel were available on the site. Lastly, concrete reduces sound transmission from room to room and is fireproof. The only parts of the Castle which are combustible are the ceilings and furnishings.

At the time the Castle was built, earthquake forces on buildings were not as well understood as they are today, but Julia Morgan with the help of faithful Walter Steilberg, both having trained as engineers, had a good intuitive grasp of structural principles.

The coverings used at Hearst Castle are varied. The ceilings were faced with wood. The walls were surfaced with cement plaster, fabric, or paneled in wood. The vestibule floors were laid-over with travertine, as was the Refectory floor. Slate flooring was used in the Gothic Lobby which gives way to the Gothic Study, and carpet was put down only occasionally, as in the Celestial Suite and the Theater, where it was used for acoustical purposes. Mosaic-tile was used rarely. In some places, namely in the Assembly Room and in the New Wing, the plaster has been scored in an almost completely uncon-

This photograph of the Assembly Room fireplace was taken in the 1930s. Mr. Hearst is said to have burned trunks of trees in it.

The Assembly Room fireplace today as seen on tours.
The Assembly Room's Great Barney Mantel from the Chateau des Jours, France. The name comes from Charles T. Barney, the
New York tycoon, in whose Park Avenue mansion this stately piece was installed at the turn of the century. Following
Barney's death, the mantel found a new home at San Simeon.

A French Gothic mantelpiece, Tuscan Gothic lanterns, Spanish choir stalls, Sienese festival banners, Italian refectory tables, Flemish Gothic tapestries — and a king's ransom in fine silver make the Refectory the most impressive of San Simeon's rooms for many visitors. William Randolph Hearst, Marion Davies, and a veritable Who's Who of 1920s and 30s luminaries dined in this elegant room.

The last major work by any of Julia Morgan's artisans (1947), these storybook murals by Camille Solon decorate a top-floor room in the New Wing.

Ever watchful, three guardian lions face westward from the balcony of the Celestial Suite.

vincing way to imitate stone work. Marble floors are covered for the most part with an outstanding collection of Oriental rugs.

Surprisingly, stained glass was not used in the Castle, which is curious for two reasons: First, because good glass was available at the time, and second, because stained glass is a hallmark of Gothic architecture.

In this chapter we have examined the buildings as objects of art in themselves. The buildings were designed to perform a number of functions. For the tourist, since he or she does not live in the Castle, work at it, or enjoy the entertainments of the past, the most important function is that of "containing," like a great concrete safe, the art objects which Mr. Hearst collected from the world markets.

Visitors to the Castle sometimes ask the Guides why La Casa Grande has not been "finished" by the State. There are several reasons which come to mind. Three stand out:

What was the finished Castle intended to look like? The fascination with the Castle for Mr. Hearst surely lay in the fact that it was never intended to be completed. It was constantly evolving in his mind, growing, as it were.

Leaving it the way Mr. Hearst left it, we have a valuable document in concrete of Julia Morgan's and Mr. Hearst's exact intentions up to the point in time they left it.

A bronze sculpture of "Anacreon," the Greek poet, by the nineteenth century French artist Jean Leon Gerome (Lower South Duplex).

One of four duplex suites in La Casa Grande. The bath and bedroom occupy one end of the suite, leaving the sitting room a two-story space.

Mural paintings and gilt details decorate a doorway in the Celestial Suite.

One of two tower rooms in the main part of La Casa Grande: the North Celestial Bedroom. The walls are hung with gold damask drapery.

Wearing a bodice of acanthus leaves and a Spanish-style corbel for a hat, a plaster of Paris caryatid stands Amazon-like in San Simeon's fifty-seat Theater.

C H A P T E R 7

THE COLLECTION

"There are no masterpieces at Hearst Castle." This remark was made by an art historian who teaches at a reputable university in California. We have no wish to quarrel with an otherwise perceptive instructor, but we assure you that his vision here is narrow.

Certainly if "masterpieces" are defined as paintings equal to a Rembrandt or a Matisse, then the Hearst collection falls a bit short. On the other hand, any collection which includes one hundred and fifty examples of Greek vases, superb tapestries, and authenticated works by Canova and Gerome must have its masterpieces. (Burton B. Fredericksen's catalogue, *Handbook of the Paintings in the Hearst San Simeon State Historical Monument,* lists eighty-nine Italian, French, Spanish, German,

Flemish and Dutch paintings.) Indeed, if our definition of a masterpiece is broadened to include Spanish wood ceilings, an art form in which Spain excelled, then Hearst Castle is rich in masterpieces.

On the other hand, it must be admitted that the Hearst collection was not put together by a professional art connoisseur like Bernard Berenson, and while the collection lacks the choice pieces found in the Frick, the Gardner, or the Getty, the works found at the Castle today accurately reflect Mr. Hearst's personal taste. The works should be viewed as a whole — as a key to the personality of the man himself, a man raised by a strong-willed and opinionated mother who had Victorian standards which she applied to the world of art and architecture.

The south alcove of the Library. The Greek vases on the plate rail above the bookshelves are but a fraction of the great number in the collection. The coffered ceiling is Spanish of the sixteenth century.

Second Empire bronze group representing "Minerva" by Emmanuel Fremiet (Library).

These standards were passed on to her son.

Burton Fredericksen, curator of paintings at the J. Paul Getty Museum, when compiling the only handbook published on the artwork housed in the Castle, expressed the opinion that most of the artwork was exhibited to conform with the interior decor. But, he goes on to say, "Many of them (works of art) are in fact of excellent quality and deserving of attention. Many are of museum quality." Mr. Fredericksen feels that due to the number and diversity of art objects on the hilltop, the Castle "contains enough fine art to make a very good small museum."

Comparing the Hearst collection to others has limited meaning. In the range and breadth of its categories it is unique. Museum quality works were not a prime requirement from Mr. Hearst's point of view. Content, color, possible future location, and selling price were all considerations for the purchase of any work of art acquired by Mr. Hearst. It is the positioning of each, and its surrounding architectural components, which accomplish the desired decorating effect, not the quality or value of the individual item. It was Miss Morgan's talents and Mr. Hearst's visions which synchronized the vast collection and its architectural components into a residence which was livable. The dryness of a museum is lacking. The furniture, antique or not, is usable; the artwork, classic or not, is decorative; and the architectural components, whether they be fifteenth century

Spanish or constructed on the hilltop, all combine to make Mr. Hearst's concrete dream a reality.

W.A. Swanberg states that Mr. Hearst . . . "became known to dealers in Europe and America as the world's premier pushover. It was understood everywhere that he could not take a normal view toward art, could not appraise a piece according to its cold market value, set a top price and stick to it . . ." When he bid for something, it was with the idea that he must have it. The thought of losing the piece to another bidder was sheer anguish. "The fact that Mr. Hearst collected or amassed objects in almost all categories astounded dealers." Swanberg says that what whetted the dealers' appetite, "was the promiscuity of his buying. Most collectors specialized, but he was interested in everything from howdahs to reliquaries, and he seemed gripped by an uncontrolled urge to buy, buy, buy." Fredericksen calls Mr. Hearst ". . . a prodigious collector, of a nature one now calls compulsive."

By about 1926, Mr. Hearst's purchases accounted for a large part of the international market. His personal holdings in art must have been larger in the 1930s than any other private collection in the United States. Most of it was never on display and certainly the entire collection was never completely cataloged, let alone subjected to curatorial scrutiny. A master inventory of the collection exists; however it is not "critical" and it is more clerical than anything else. Apart from what was dis-

Harlequin lamp in the Art Deco style of the 1920s
(Billiard Room).

Chinese vase-lamp formerly in the Beach House collection of
Marion Davies (New Wing).

played in the Castle in 1939, art objects were housed in the San Simeon warehouses, the huge Bronx warehouse, the "Hacienda" at Pleasanton, the residence at Wyntoon on the McCloud River, the Beach House in Santa Monica, St. Donat's Castle in Wales, the Bibicora Ranch in Mexico, and the numerous other abodes Mr. Hearst possessed.

One can understand the depression in the world art market when, in 1937, Mr. Hearst was forced, by financial problems, to stop buying and to start selling. By the mid 1930s, he had probably spent over fifty million dollars on art. The art liquidation took many forms. Individual items like St. Donat's Castle went on the market, and some items were sold through art dealers to collector-clients. A large number of items were sold on the fifth floor of Gimbel's Department store in New York. A deal was made whereby Saks Fifth Avenue handled the paintings (Van Dyck, Gainsborough, Murillo and others), while Gimbels handled the rest (furniture, vases, statues, and so forth). The advertisements read "Bargains in Del Sartos and Broadlooms", and everyone came looking and buying. The sale lasted for eight years and was an unqualified success.

The art objects on view at Hearst Castle lack examples of many types of art Mr. Hearst had collected, such as stained glass and suits of armor. Measured by volume, the works of art now at the Castle possibly represent one-tenth of his total holdings. Mr. Hearst appears to have started his collecting in

In the corner of the Billiard Room stands an Atwater Kent radio in
1920s Gothic style.

Game tables repose under a Spanish Gothic ceiling; the French hunting tapestry is of the ''Mille-Fleur,'' or thousand flower variety (Billiard Room).

''The Engagement of Hasdrubal'' is one of four monumental tapestries illustrating the ''Deeds of Scipio Africanus,'' the Roman general who led his forces to victory over Hannibal and the Carthaginians in 202 B.C. (Assembly Room).

Focal point of the Billiard Room is this late fifteenth or early sixteenth century French tapestry of ''Mille-Fleur''
design. The scene depicts a stag hunt well in progress. There may have been other tapestries of similar
size and design showing the same hunt in earlier and later stages; if so, this is the sole survivor — no other tapestries of
closely matching composition are known to exist today.

Fragment of a Graeco-Roman statue
(Assembly Room).

"Portrait of Alvisius Vendramin" by Jacopo Tintoretto (Doge's
Sitting Room).

Grandest by far of San Simeon's numerous guest quarters is the Doge's Suite in La Casa Grande. Silk damask wall hangings
and mostly Italian furnishing and decorations convey the atmosphere of a sixteenth century Renaissance palazzo.

Rare Urbino majolica inkstand of the sixteenth century. The original user of the piece provided St. George with a dragon-slaying spear in the form of a writing implement (Doge's Sitting Room).

One of the most medieval, castle-like rooms is the Morning Room, just behind the Refectory and adjacent to the Kitchen and Pantry. The Gothic mantelpiece is from a French chateau.

1894 and he continued acquiring until the mid-1940s. The value of the collection lies not in the intrinsic worth of the holdings, but in the selection process by which they came to coexist. Looked at from this perspective, we discover that a strong unity exists. The apparent diversity has a unity which centers on Mr. Hearst himself.

Because the collection and the art objects in it have an intrinsic meaning independent of their location and another meaning in terms of their environment and proximity to other objects, we will exam them in two ways. First, we will see them in terms of their position in the Castle and then on a thematic basis in groups.

Main Vestibule

Most people enter the Castle proper or La Casa Grande by the Main Vestibule which is extremely narrow and excessively high. The Roman mosaic floor cannot be fully appreciated as it is partly covered with tour mats. Uncovered portions should be examined as closely as time permits. The mosaic is authentic Roman and comparable to those seen in Italy. The mosaic would not have been particularly remarkable in Rome, for this was a typical flooring material for public buildings and upper class houses. The Vestibule marble mosaic is circa first century B.C. The center section, which is the visible part, is entitled ''Merman and Fishes.''

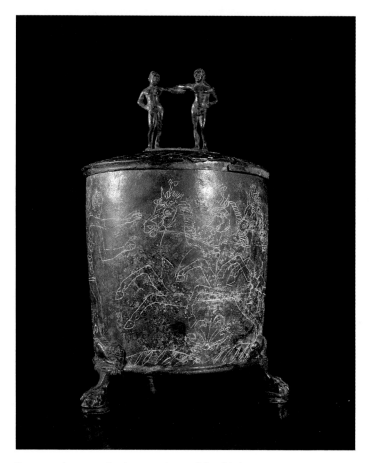

Etruscan cista, or toiletries container, of the third century B.C. (Library).

A seated woman, one of two Greek Tánagra figures.

Terra cotta bust of a Florentine church dignitary in the Library Lobby.

Looking to the right and then to the left we see, respectively, two marble statues. The statues are backed by two tapestries, one of which is from Phoebe Apperson Hearst's collection. The statue to the right appears to be a rather silly woman seemingly cavorting around. She is called "Enchante" and she was made by American sculptor Fredrick MacMonnies in 1914. The original was done in bronze and is in the Metropolitan Museum in New York. The lady is balanced on one foot and looks inebriated. She appears to be at odds with the rather scenic environment. Behind her hangs an armorial tapestry dated 1684 and done for the Spanish Ayala Family, after drawings by David Teniers.

To the left we encounter a Carrara marble statue group on the familiar theme of "Pygmalion and Galatea" by Jean Léon Gérôme, a nineteenth century French sculptor and painter. His bronze statue of Anacreon is in the Lower South Duplex and his paintings of Napoleon, in the Celestial Suite, are far superior.

On the wall behind the statue hangs a Gobelin tapestry from the Phoebe Hearst collection. Several sets of the design by Lebrun were woven when he was at the Gobelin factory in France. The set was entitled "History of Alexander." The inscription on this tapestry says "Alexander Sacerdotibus Benedictionem Accipit", which means "Alexander receives blessing from the Priests."

In the fleeting moments allotted to the Vestibule, the visitor's time should be spent examining the excellent marble door frame, pieced to fit and of high quality by a member of the famed Sansovini family who made such a great contribution to the architecture of Renaissance Venice. Note especially the carving on the shaft of the columns and the subtle cornice above. The coat of arms of Pope Julius II (1503 – 1513) is found on the doorway. Pope Julius was a patron of the arts and started the rebuilding of St. Peters in Rome. He was also a patron of Michelangelo and Raphael.

The Assembly Room, Refectory, and Morning Room

These three rooms have been discussed in some detail in Chapter Six. All contain many objects of interest, but the pace of the tour makes detailed inspection impossible.

The Assembly Room overwhelms first-time visitors. It presents an almost insurmountable problem: What to look at? The authors suggest the visitor look first at the overall room. Remember it is not a museum, but it is the residence of one man and his guests. After absorbing the general feeling of the room, pick out several objects that interest you, the tapestries, statues, furniture, fireplace, paintings, or choir stalls. They are all excellent choices. If you look straight ahead to the center of the room you will see a beautiful rock crystal presentation case or reclining Italian bronze figures of "River Gods" by Niccolo Pericoli (1500 – 1565) on a shining sixteenth century Italian

William Randolph Hearst's bedroom. A rare Persian jar is on the night table and the framed di Buoninsegna painting sits on the chest in this early photograph.

walnut table. Directly beyond the table is the rather imposing fireplace.

To the visitors' left is the north end of the room, with its bronze figure "Drinking Nymph" by V. Seifert on the center of the table. In the corners are a statue of Venus by Antonio Canova and a fragmentary torso of another Venus. Presumably this marble is a genuine antique from the time of the Roman Empire. If this is true, it is the oldest object in the room. Displayed at a distance so far removed from the visitors' path, it is impossible to view it closely. Above the window is a life-size marble head of Faustinas, the wife of Marcus Aurelius, the Roman Emperor.

Glancing to the South end of the room reveals a Wurlitzer electric player piano, and a large opened parchment book. The Gregorian chant book was hand lettered in 1826. The book is bound in leather and measures about thirty by twenty-four inches. Also at this end of the room and close to the path of the tour mat stands the bronze figure "The Setting Sun" by Adolf A. Weinemann, an American (1914). This figure is a copy done at a reduced scale of the statue, commissioned in 1914, which adorned the Court of the Universe at the Panama-Pacific Exposition in San Francisco in 1915. The full scale model was popularly called "Descending Night."

The Theater

The Theater, illustrated at the beginning of this chapter, does not contain any art objects but the entire room is in itself a "work of art." Fourteen huge, grotesque, humanoid female figures are seemingly pinned to the walls. They are executed in the style of the late 1920s. While staring straight ahead in a vacuous manner, their faces are aglow from the electric light bulbs held in their outstretched hands. Certainly they are not to be confused with the Athenian carytids on the Acropolis, but they do have a kinship with similar ladies done in nineteenth century in Germany, for example. In the German translation, they look more like something other than demi-goddesses of Athenian Elysian Fields.

The room also contains overstuffed theater seats, fabric walls, and a retracting screen which at one time descended into the basement below. A telephone is found next to the front left seat, the one usually occupied by Mr. Hearst. With this phone he could talk to the projectionist or use the outside line that was connected to the switchboard which functioned twenty-four hours a day. Movies were shown in the theater even before it was finished. Adela Rogers St. Johns, in her book *Honeycomb,* talks about sitting on pillows on the floor and grabbing a fur coat from a pile near the door to keep warm in the unheated theater.

Hanging below the pyramidal ceiling of Mr. Hearst's bedroom is the painting of "Madonna and Child" by Bernardino di Mariotto.

Behind the old decorated parchment lampshade is a photograph of Mr. Hearst's father, George Hearst.

The Billiard Room

Upon entering the Billiard Room the visitor is aware of being confronted by the stone wall at the far end of the room. There is a strange combination of a round arched doorway, representing Romanesque architecture, placed under vine Gothic decorative carving. The semispherical triangles incongruously formed at the sides of this wall are surfaced with one hundred Persian tiles presumably dating to the seventeenth century. The tiles illustrate a poem, "Joseph and Potiphars' Wife." The entire combination rises to meet a fifteenth century Spanish wood ceiling of Moorish persuasion. This unlikely combination fits together so well that the diversity of time and space is not apparent.

The west wall is occupied by a justly famous late medieval French tapestry. The "Mille Fleur" or thousand flower design tapestry is about 500 years old. The work depicts a hunting scene and deserves close scrutiny for both form and content. Notice that the background figures are not smaller but are placed higher in the composition. At the time this work was being finished, Italian painters like Massacio were already employing a new method of space representation called one point perspective. In terms of content, this hunting scene effectively depicts life in late medieval times.

Two more Persian tile panels, using the Gothic method of two dimensional space representation, flank the French tapestry. These enameled tile panels presumably come from the great Iranian city of Isfahan. Below the panels are two beautiful jewel chests. The one on the left is Italian and is covered with decorative metal. The other is from Limoges, France, and is decorated with enamel work.

Less obvious and easily missed because of their locations are the contemporary objects. On the right immediately upon entering is a small table lamp, less than twenty-three inches high. The figure which forms the body of the lamp is a harlequin with red shoes and a stiff cape in a kind of Bat Man costume. The table on the north wall supports an authentic Atwater Kent radio and a 1930s cradle-type black telephone, both of which brings us sharply into the early twentieth century, after the euphoria of medieval France or the Persia of Shah Abbas.

The rooms on the upper level are so numerous and rich in content that we now become highly selective in our choices for discussion. None of the items mentioned should be missed, if at all possible.

The Doge's Suite

At the present time the visitor on Tour Two is brought directly to the Doge's Suite after viewing the Neptune Pool and North Terrace. The room takes its name from the screen or grills at the outer edge of the balcony, but contains no Venetian works of art except for a painting which Fredericksen at-

Col. Willicombe's room in the Billiard Room Wing. The walls are covered with ornamental stucco.

tributes to the school of Tintoretto. "The artist, who was once thought to be Tintoretto himself, was one of Tintoretto's many followers. Bought from the dealer Goldschmidt in 1935." All of the windows of the suite look to the back court- yard and garden area and out to the Santa Lucia Mountains. The Sitting Room, which is centered in the suite, is connected to a balcony or loggia, where the ancient quatrefoil arches and old railings make up the balustrade.

Each of the bedrooms of this suite contains excellent art ob- jects. The north bedroom which is seen first contains an eight- eenth century Italian ceiling, a seventeenth century carved walnut bed, and some excellent silver repoussé sconces. A vel- vet cape or ecclesiastical vestment, with gold needlework, from late fifteenth century France adorns one of the walls of the south bedroom. Also found in this room are an English gothic forged iron lecturn from the late fifteenth century, and a pair of exquisite green jade lamps in the shape of the phoe- nix. The door framings are molded and surround seventeenth century Spanish sacristy doors. In Roman Catholic churches a sacristy room, in which sacred vessels and vestments are kept, is a small room to one side of the altar where the priests vest for Mass.

The Doge Sitting Room walls are draped with heavy blue decorative wall hanging making a rich backdrop for the multi- tude of objects found here. The ceiling, according to Freder-

icksen, the Curator at the J. Paul Getty Museum, is one of only a few of its kind known to exist. The center portion was possi- bly painted in the late seventeenth century from the school of the Flemish artist Joachim Wtewael. It represents the annuncia- tion to the shepherds of the birth of Christ. Paintings surround- ing the center panel are later work by another artist.

A tiny black basalt statuette of possible Egyptian Eighteenth Dynasty origin sits modestly on the table looking more like a papeweight than a god. The visitor should try not to miss the ceramic inkwell of St. George flanked by two jars of sixteenth century Majolica ware from Italy (Urbino). Saint George sits on his horse atop a stand containing secret drawers. His lance, a plumed pen, is no longer in his right hand.

Our personal favorite is the bronze copy of Apollo and Daphne by Gianlorenzo Bernini. The Baroque sculptors in Italy were the first to experiment with movement. This piece shows Apollo, on Daphne's trail, closing in on her as she turns herself into a laurel tree. The statue is poorly placed. It is usually sur- rounded by people on the tour and the guide cannot ade- quately explain its importance. It also stands against a lighted window which makes it all the more difficult to view.

The Cloisters

Moving to the next level, the second story at the front of

the Castle, the third story at the back (due to higher ceilings in the major rooms below), we pass a series of rooms known as the Cloisters because they do not open directly to an inside corridor but to flanking passages or cloisters. The tours generally do not enter these rooms and the tourist must be content with glancing through the doors or windows. At this point we become aware of the extent of the rich collection, of major importance, of Spanish vargueños and papeleiras. Many drawers in these chests are inlaid with ivory and polychromed. The cabinets are carved in high relief and the vargueños have doors that hinge at the bottom, forming a cover when not in use and a desk top when opened.

Each of the three Cloister Rooms has some interesting items. The first room on the tour (actually Cloister Number Three), and the next both have some pieces by the Della Robbia family. The last bedroom along the cloister has an English Gothic alabaster mantle which is carved with figures of nine saints.

The Library

The passages flanking the Cloister Rooms are directly over the Refectory and lead to the Library over the Assembly Room. This room contains a wealth of books, over 4,500 volumes on all subjects. All of the volumes were printed before the 1940s. Below the shelves are cupboards with a number of large bound volumes, most relating to fine art classification. On the left side of the room, or south alcove, the shelves contain a mixture of fiction and nonfiction by English, American and German philosophers and novelists. The north alcove contains the volumes on history, biography and collected (published) autographs of noted persons. The rare books are found in the center section of the room. The art books, those on religion, science, wildlife, and reference works are also found in this area.

The pointed arches of the Gothic Study are decorated with paintings by Camille Solon. The kindest thing that can be said about them is that the room would have been infinitely better without them. The Study itself contains a wealth of really fine objects, some of which are very tiny, shown in glass lighted cases under the bookshelves. The other works of art are too numerous to be seen on tour. One must choose quickly between Persian jars, ivory tankards from Holland and Germany, a Russian tankard, a Sheffield silver wax jack, a silver Dutch drinking cup, and a pair of bronze Venetian lions. The top shelf on the bookcase supports a remarkable diversity of objects, among them a Venetian iron rooster flag holder, a number of Spanish reliquary busts, and a Spanish statue of St. Ann, Virgin, and Child. Our advice is to ignore all this in favor of a handsome Gothic chimney piece with flanking Gothic doorways, a choice German clock from Augsberg, barely visible at the end of the room, and, of course, a pair of glass and metal lamps that are shaped like domed buildings which make for one of

This New Wing fourth floor bathroom is the largest in the Castle. In tan marble, it is 36½ feet long.

the truly unique possessions of the Collection.

The Gothic Study, like the Library, abounds with books on many subjects. The more than 7,500 volumes fall into four major classifications: history, biography, philosophy, and fine arts. There is also a collection of special bound and limited editions, many with uncut pages. Childrens' books are located along the North wall.

A visual tour of the room brings us to the focal point of the whole room, a portrait of a youthful Mr. Hearst painted by Orrin Peck, an early friend, the best man at his wedding, and beneficiary of his mother's assistance. Few artists have a work hanging in such a commanding location. Unfortunately, Mr. Peck died in 1921 and never saw his work displayed at the heart, so to speak, of Mr. Hearst's empire.

Beyond the Gothic Study facing the eastern mountains is Mr. Hearst's private office, the center of gravity of the whole hilltop complex. Because it is such a personal place, we feel the presence of this powerful, enigmatic man. His chair seems to be larger than most, maybe to accommodate his grander than six-foot frame. The backdrop of the mountains, as seen behind his chair, must have had an imposing effect on those commanded to appear there. At the present Mr. Hearst's private offices are not on any tour; perhaps that may change in time.

In his own bedroom—despite the presence of the unique

This stunning and dramatic bathroom on the second floor of the New Wing has white marble walls and black fixtures.

ceiling from southern (Teruel) Spain, the Persian jar sitting casually on the night table, and a choice Italian painting with possible attribution to Duccio di Buoninsegna hanging on the South wall—what attracts us to this room are the personal mementos. The painting was a gift to Mr. Hearst from Eleanor "Cissy" Paterson, publisher of the *Washington Times-Herald* in 1932. These include photographs of his father, an indifferent oil painting of his mother, a framed poem called *La Cuesta Encantada* from the *Lady of Lyons* by Bulwer Lytton, and a poem of his own in the form of a book plate. Actually, the personal trinkets are few in number and it can only be assumed that most of the others were removed after his departure to Beverly Hills when he was terminally ill.

In addition to the collection of books, the room contains an inordinate number of art objects, as does the entrance corridor outside. Within the Library is housed Mr. Hearst's entire collection of Greek vases casually displayed in a plate rail above the bookcases. Other objects of art, including part of the vase collection, are contained in lighted cases below the bookcase. This rare and outstanding collection of Greek vases will be examined in more detail later. The ceiling is noteworthy architecturally, but of passing interest to most visitors. It is re-

constructed of three ceilings (originally of a total group of seven) from the sixteenth century state apartments of Castle Benies, Spain. The fifteenth century Italian mantel is from the town of Fiesole in Tuscany. The mantel is a unique example of the low-relief carving of Benedetto da Maiano. But the fireplace and mantel appear too large for the room.

The North alcove, to the right on entering, contains a bronze Etruscan cista, possibly from the third century B.C. The cista is a simple cylinder with feet and a lid with a tiny statuette of a man and a woman. The sides of the cylinder are engraved with lines showing Aphrodite in her chariot drawn by four horses. Note the assurance and authority with which the unknown artist worked, linking the work to that of other master draftsmen like Matisse and Picasso.

While still near the North alcove, the visitor should glance at the two pieces of sixteenth century Italian furniture. The cabinet-type table has an octagonal top and a rectangular base. The Savonarola folding chair is near the window.

In the South alcove we are drawn to a gilded bronze sculptural group, three horses pulling a chariot driven by a woman. Minerva, Goddess of Wisdom, is going out to do battle against ignorance and lust. The group is by a French artist of the nineteenth century, Emmanuel Fremiet. What an interesting attempt to reinforce a statement about contemporary virtue with a link to classical imagery! Minerva was the daughter of Jupiter. She presided over the useful and ornamenal arts, both those of men, such as agriculture and navigation, and those of women, such as spinning, weaving and needlework. Athens was her chosen seat and the city was named for her, Athene. A masterpiece? Hardly. Yet it serves to give us an insight into French art of the Second Empire.

The Library Lobby contains a fine terra cotta bust of a Florentine church dignitary. Those of us who frequent the Castle are often stuck by his strange expression, a combination of wisdom, weariness, and wit. He seems poised, ready to speak out as he stares at us silently, his forehead wrinkled, and his brow furrowed. One wonders if he has just finished a perplexing conversation on the 1920s-style phone which rests nearby.

The Third Level and Mr. Hearst's Rooms

Immediately above the Library is the heart of the Castle. We are now on the third level above ground. This part of the Castle was reserved for Mr. Hearst himself. Two bedrooms, separated by a low-ceilinged sitting room which faces west, are linked to the Gothic Study by a vestibule containing the most significant artifact in the Castle for Mr. Hearst — a newspaper rack. Here he had at hand the daily editions of his newspapers.

The Sitting Room, which both connects and separates Mr. Hearst's private bedroom from the North Gothic bedroom, is solidly packed with beautiful objects. Our interest in a beautiful chest covered with gold leaf is heightened when we learn that he kept his hats in it. The room contains about forty major items, too many to examine in detail on tour. Fifteen of these are statues from Spain, Italy, Alsace, France, Flanders, and Germany. Five of the statues are of St. Barbara, either by coincidence or by design, and people may attempt to infer something about Mr. Hearst from this. (Saint Barbara was locked in the tower of a castle for her faith. Perhaps a fiction, she is no longer thought to have existed.) To the left of the door leading to the north bedroom hangs a fine early Italian painting from Northern Italy. The painting is exceptionally large, of oil glazes on wood panels. The color has a jewel-like brilliance. Close to the viewer, the painting can be studied in detail.

The north bedroom contains a ceiling similar in shape to the one in Mr. Hearst's bedroom. It is equally beautiful but, whereas the former is figurative from Christian Spain, this one is geometric and more typical of Moorish Spain. It was constructed in the fifteenth century for Castle Marchino, according to the Castle inventory card. The walls of this room are hung with eight distinguished paintings of the fourteenth and fifteenth centuries from various parts of Italy, a remarkably consistent group. There are also two Spanish varqueños, a pair

of Chinese carved rose quartz lamps, Austrian silver sconces, and a bronze bas-relief by Antonio Averlino, called "Il Filerete." He was one of the most important architects of the early Renaissance in Northern Italy.

The New Wing

The floor of rooms above the Theater is known as the New Wing because it was constructed later than the Castle proper. One has the feeling here that, although Mr. Hearst ordered the work done, he did not have the same interest in the result. Ironically, some of the most choice possessions of the collection are found here.

We climb to the second floor of the New Wing to gain access to the room usually occupied by Col. Willicombe. (The room is actually in the older part of the Castle above the Billiard Room.) The countertop, walls, and ceiling of the dressing table are covered with a beautiful amber glass. Looking up provides a kaleidoscope of never-ending visions.

The Bathrooms

In some respects, the best examples of contemporary Art Deco style at the Castle are the bathrooms in the New Wing. If the designer (for Julia Morgan had assistance at this point), was hesitant in the treatment of the period rooms, he was truly at home in the bathrooms. These rooms have confidence and take their place with the great central California Coast facilities such as those at the Madonna Inn and the Monday Club of San Luis Obispo (also by Julia Morgan) on upper Monterey Street.

The photographs included here give only a hint of the richness and variety of Hearst Castle bathrooms. The largest is on the top floor. This singular bathroom is thirty-six and one half feet long and was planned originally as an open corridor directly over the corridor two floors below. The bathroom is entirely faced with a rich tan marble and was not finished until 1947.

The major bathrooms on the floor immediately below are lined with white marble and edged with black strips on the floor, walls, and in the shower. Someone must have decided to do something stylish. The fixtures are shiny jet black. They fit the New Wing whose walls are plaster, made to look like stone. The windows have screens and fabric-covered oversized valance boxes. Suddenly we feel ourselves in a modern building containing art objects, somewhat like a museum. The bathrooms reinforce this feeling. Subtle integration of the old and new is missing.

The Kitchen

Returning to the first floor, we find the Kitchen. The rich

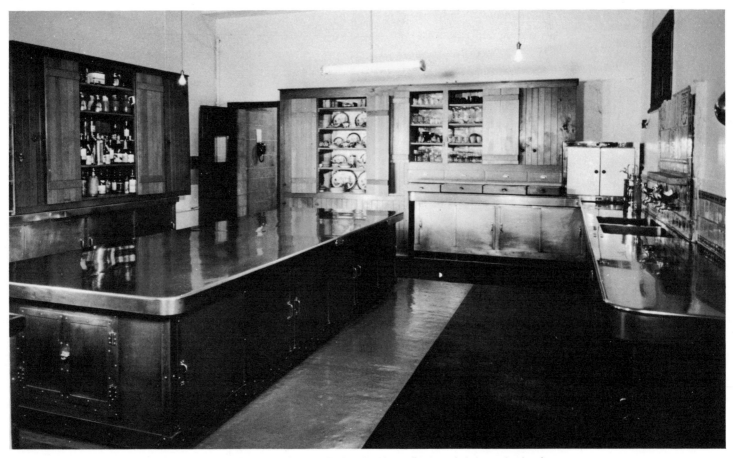

The Pantry. "Monel metal" countertops; antique plates and glass are displayed with a collection of vintage wine bottles.

metal surfaces are not aluminum, but a kind of stainless steel called "Monel metal." Tile over the counters on the east wall carry the motto "Sine Ipso Fact V. Est Nihil" (Without Him There Is Nothing). This is sometimes thought to be a reference to Mr. Hearst himself. The tiles are copies of an original in the Casa del Monte ("B" House), which is said to be a family motto on the coat of arms of the Zuniga family in Spain. The motto recalls the biblical statement in the first chapter of the Book of Revelations of St. John the Divine: "All things were made by Him and without Him nothing that was made."

The Kitchen area is divided into two parts, the Pantry and the Kitchen proper. The exposed concrete trusses in the ceiling will delight the curious and the vintage kitchen equipment will engage those interested in industrial design. On the other hand, the antiquarian will delight in Phoebe Apperson Hearst's Gosham silver-plated flatware. Note especially the "marrow scoops" and Booth's authentic old silicon ware from England. Connoisseurs can examine a selection of wine bottles retrieved from the basement by the present housekeeping staff.

The Pantry is twenty-four by fifty-one foot and the Kitchen is twenty-two feet eight inches by thirty feet six inches. It contains an oil burning range, the baking ovens, four warming ovens, bread and roll warmer, steamer, steam pressure kettle, charcoal broiler, electric utensils and chopping block. The only apparent "art objects" are the curious brass birds that form the handles of the faucets.

Highly polished brass birds adorn the faucets in the kitchen.

One of the sloping sides of the rare, fourteenth century Spanish ceiling drops in William Randolph Hearst's private bedroom.

A 1930s craftsman-made ceiling of plaster, wood, and paint and gilt decoration (Celestial Suite).

The domestic staff in Mr. Hearst's day included a butler, assistant butler, waiters or waitresses, a chef, a second chef, a cook's helper, a pastry cook, an apprentice cook and a dishwasher. Additional help was brought in from Los Angeles at times.

Having discussed the diversity that exists in nearly every room, we are now ready to turn our attention to particular groupings within the collection, independent of their individual locations.

As mentioned throughout the text, the ceilings are a special treasure of Hearst Castle. We recall no other museum or castle in the world where they are comparable.

As a group, the ceilings of the Castle proper and the guest houses constitute the most unique part of Mr. Hearst's collection. The antique wood ceilings are suspended on wires from the concrete structure above. In general, the ceilings of the guest houses are cast in plaster of Paris in sections from designs by Julia Morgan and are painted to imitate carved wood. The ceilings of La Casa Grande (except for the Kitchen, which expresses the concrete structure), are for the most part antiques from Spain or Italy, frequently pieced to fit the room. Most of the painted ceilings are from Spain, since the Spaniards excelled in this category of art. Mr. Hearst's primary art connoisseur in Spain was Arthur Byne, who wrote a fine book entitled *Decorated Wood Ceilings of Spain*. It was largely due to Mr. Byne's connections that Mr. Hearst was able to acquire

The "Salamanca" ceiling — a sixteenth century Spanish example in carved, painted, and gilded wood (New Wing).

An ingenious combination of two French paintings, a set of Spanish armorial tondos, fragments of a Venetian cornice, and 1930s plaster and woodwork in the ceiling of the Lower South Duplex.

such a brilliant collection of Spanish work.

On the lower floor one need not linger in studying the Assembly Room ceiling. Poor lighting and patching render it difficult to see. The vestibule alcove is a far better and a brilliant piece of decorative design.

The Refectory ceiling is problematic. The inventory lists the work as Italian. However, this is uncertain. The ceiling contains fifteen nearly life-size figures of saints placed in deep coffers and all in natural wood. The whole design is so curious and unusual that some authorities believe it was originally not a ceiling at all, but was perhaps mounted vertically as it would be in a reredos behind an altar. This idea raises more problems than it solves. The saint most immediately recognizable is the Virgin in the center panel. Her primacy is underscored not only by her central position, but by the angels in the corners. St. George is in the center panel immediately to the east, complete with horse, spear and dragon. St. Barbara with her tower can be found placed near the east wall, while St. Christopher and St. Petronius, the patron saint of Bologna, can be recognized. St. Petronius is holding what appears to be a model of three churches. This is the only figurative sculptured ceiling and is a major treasure, despite its unknown origin.

The remaining major lower floor ceilings, except for the Theater, are antiques from Spain containing elements of Moorish design. Moorish inspired wood ceilings are non-sculptural,

One of several larger-than-life-sized figures — in this case a representation of St. Petronius — in the Refectory's gigantic ceiling.

The famous "Cardinal Richelieu Bed" in La Casa del Monte. The coat of arms in the headboard is of the Boffa family of Lombardy, Italy. Behind the bed hangs a Flemish armorial tapestry of the 1600s.

Jewel cabinet with insets of Limoges medallions — French, 1562 (Billiard Room).

involving intricate geometric decoration. When passing down the corridor leading from the Morning Room to the Billiard Room, the high corridor windows in the interior wall open to a wash room with a lovely ceiling in brilliant color and delicate scale.

The ceilings of the remaining upstairs rooms are too numerous to discuss individually, but each is worthy of attention. Most are from Spain.

Mr. Hearst's private bedroom has a ceiling in the form of a truncated pyramid, certainly an outstanding example of early Spanish art of the fourteenth century. The ceiling contains fifty-three panels or coffers, each with painted figures of saints. The lighting here is only adequate, though sufficient to see the figures which should be studied in detail. The ceiling comes from the town of Teruel in the province of Aragon, Spain. Four other ceilings like it are known to exist. One is in Florence, two more in Spain, and the other is in Santa Barbara, California.

A ceiling of great delicacy and charm is in the South Lower Duplex. It includes oil on canvas paintings of "Endymion" and the "Departure of Phoebus" by the French painter Jean-Baptiste Van Loo, 1684–1745. Finishing off the ceiling are four pair of armorial tondi from the Spanish Renaissance. The visitor is offered a unique opportunity to view this ceiling. When in the upper room of the Duplex, "Endymion" is directly over the bed. While in the lower level of the Duplex, the visitor should

The last of the major rooms built at San Simeon — and unquestionably one of the finest in a long line of
Hearst-Morgan productions — is the third-floor Gothic Study, the innermost sanctum of Mr. Hearst himself.
A profusion of medieval and Renaissance objects and furnishings, including mural and bookcase work by Julia Morgan's
master craftsmen, are among the highlights of the room.

The stateliness of Renaissance art; a sixteenth-century Italian credenza. (Assembly Room).

Italian Renaissance Dante chair in inlaid holly wood (New Wing).

walk to the far wall and look up to see the entire ceiling.

Endymion was a beautiful youth who fed his flock of sheep on Mount Latmos. Jupiter bestowed on him the gift of perpetual youth united with perpetual sleep. The story of Endymion suggests aspiring and poetic love, a life spent more in dreams than in reality and an early and welcome death. Phoebus, which means bright, is usually remembered as Phoebus Apollo, the god of archery, prophecy, and music. The two painted canvases originally hung on each side of the Assembly Room fireplace.

The last ceiling selected for special mention is on the fourth floor of the New Wing. This room is a treasure house of art objects, but the ceiling is also suprisingly high. It is in the form of a truncated pyramid, and again the lighting is poor. In contrast to the one in Mr. Hearst's bedroom, the ceiling's pyramidal shape referred to as Moorish "Salamanca," extends very high in the air. Such a shape is possible only on the upper floor where the attic can receive the height. Note especially the interlacing of the wood forms at the top and the zigzag pattern at the corners of the pyramid. This is truly a masterpiece and worth the whole tour to see. The center of the ceiling forms into the shape of a stalactite from which hangs a metal lantern.

Of all the precious furniture pieces in the Castle, the authors have chosen a few to suggest the richness of the whole.

The jewel case at the north end of the Billiard Room is especially beautiful because of the pictorial enamel medallion set

Cupids and garlands add a whimsical note in slipcovered chairs and sofas (Assembly Room).

Terra cotta bust of a young boy. School of the Florentine master Andrea Della Robbia (Della Robbia Room).

in ebony. The enamel work is from Limoges, France, and bears the date of 1562. At this time France was undergoing a transition from medieval ideas and usages to the Renaissance, under considerable influence from Italy. Limoges artisans were famous throughout the western world for their skill in developing decorative enamel work.

Chairs range from beautifully carved choir stalls, previously mentioned, to nondescript, overstuffed, formless seats that were typical of the period. The Assembly Room chairs were covered in a material especially made to match the frolicking children on the borders of the Giulio Romano tapestries. The covers were woven by Scalamandre's of New York in the late 1940s. It is as interesting as it is unsuccessful, complicating an already complex area. There is no doubt that Mr. Hearst authorized this fabric cover himself.

There are various kinds of wooden chairs on the hilltop. Dante chairs are found in the Refectory. This set of forty-eight (twenty-two are on display), is of walnut, with seats and backs of leather covered with Italian velvet in a pomegranate design. This design is known as the "Velvet of the Doges." A Dante chair folds similarly to a modern camp chair. Another type of folding chair can be found in the Library, and in the north alcove is a Savonarola folding chair presumably dating to the sixteenth century.

An intricately decorated wooden chair can be seen in the New Wing, fourth floor, (now in the last bedroom on the tour). It is a sixteenth century Florentine chair of double "V" shape construction. This Dantesque shaped chair is decorated with certosina work. Chairs with tapestry seats can also be seen. In room two of the third floor in New Wing there are two tapestry covered armchairs called "caquetoire." These French Renaissance chairs were used by women for gossiping and chatting.

Still other kinds of seating abound at the Castle. There is a settee and five chairs from eighteenth century France in the same room as the previously mentioned caquetoire. The settee and chairs are from the Regency Period, have gilt frames, and are covered in silk needlepoint.

One can also see stunning examples of papeleras, varguenos, credenzas, trunks, cassoni, and tables. A papelera is a Moorish chest that takes its name from the Spanish word for paper, *papel,* a kind of early filing cabinet. They usually have a large number of drawers and cupboards. Because of the Moorish influence the decorations are elaborate, geometric inlays. Papeleras can be found in several rooms and hallways.

The credenza or sideboard received its name from Italian food testers. Because of numerous food poisoning attempts, testers were used extensively in the fifteenth, sixteenth and seventeenth centuries. The tester would stand at the sideboard and test the food by smell and other ways known only to him. He would then give credence to it, hence the name credenza. Examples are found in the Library Lobby and the

"St. Joseph and the Child" flanked by angel candleholders — Della Robbia sculptures (Della Robbia Room).

entry hall of second floor New Wing. Credenzas are usually elbow height and have large cupboards below.

Several types of chests and trunks are to be found here also. These include marriage chests and leather or wood trunks. The marriage chests have hinged lids and are usually fitted on the inside. In the fourth bedroom of Casa del Sol is a painted fifteenth century Gothic marriage chest, with hinged lid and front. The interior is fitted with drawers and trays. Other furniture naturally includes chests of drawers, beds, bedside tables, stools, prayer benches, cabinets, and framed mirrors.

The work of the Della Robbia family of Renaissance Italy is found in various locations in the Castle, but tends to be concentrated in the Della Robbia Room immediately above the Doge's Suite. On entering the room, pay particular attention to the small bust of a child. Portraying children as children in art was almost an invention of the Renaissance, and the first Renaissance building on the streets of Florence was the Foundling Hospital designed by Filippo Brunelleschi and graced by the famous circular medallions of full-figured child by Andrea Della Robbia.

At Hearst Castle we can stand quite close to this object placed in the middle of the bureau. On the mantel is a relief of St. Joseph and child. The Della Robbia family is represented elsewhere as well, such as in the wreath found above the mantel in the Doge's Suite.

"Pygmalion and Galatea" by Jean Leon Gerome (Main Vestibule).

"The Venus of Canova" by the Neoclassic master Antonio Canova (Assembly Room).

A copy in bronze of Bernini's "Apollo and Daphne." Artist unknown (Doge's Sitting Room).

"Enchante" by the American sculptor Frederick MacMonnies (Main Vestibule).

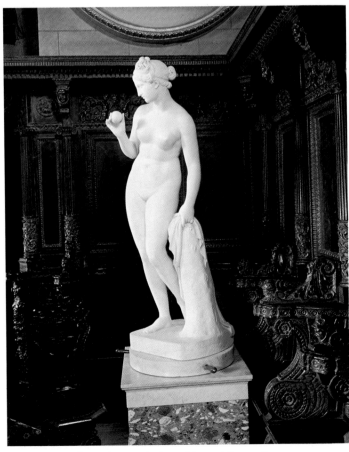

"Venus Triumphant" by Bertol Thorvaldsen of Denmark (Assembly Room).

For the visitor who is not an art historian, the identification of classical and neoclassical work poses a problem. Classical sculpture refers to original work produced in ancient Greece and Rome. Neoclassical sculpture refers to many things, but is commonly used to describe eighteenth or nineteenth century sculpture inspired by classical work. Both classical and neo-classical work is frequently copied from earlier originals which have been lost or destroyed. This practice has continued right into the twentieth century, at least at Hearst Castle. Classical sculpture, usually in the form of copies in bronze or marble, exists inside and outside the Castle. Neoclassical sculpture in marble and bronze in the form of originals and copies can be found inside the castle. Roman sarcophagi made of limestone grace the garden in various locations. Not all of them are seen on any one tour, and not all of them are authentic. Some are possible forgeries. Various styles of carving are illustrated, the most arresting example in front of Casa del Monte showing the nine muses and made of marble. Note the deep undercut-ting characteristics of late Roman work, as opposed to the shallow relief at the ends. More classic is the sarcophagus in front of Casa del Mar which shows figures paying homage to Demeter or Ceres, goddess of fertility. Note also that Deme-ter is seated in front of a representation of a four column (tetrostyle) temple. This sarcophagus is much worn and must have been sharper when first carved. The delicacy of the fig-ures and the handling of the drapery, as well as the composi-

Largest and most imposing of San Simeon 's rooms, the Assembly Room is a treasure house of architectural objects as well as decorative and fine arts. To the right of the Great Barney Mantel is one of Giulio Romano's tapestries from the ''Deeds of Scipio Afriacanus'' set; above the window is a seventeenth-century Brussels weaving of ''Neptune and Venus.'' Thorvaldsen's ''Venus Triumphant'' along with two of the sames artists' Neoclassic medallions decorate the south alcove. In the foreground, slipcovered chairs appropriate to life at ''the Ranch.''

Eighteenth century majolica pitcher converted to an electric lamp (New Wing).

Grecian askos of the fifth century B.C. (Library).

tion, indicate that it may have been carved by a Greek in Roman times. (On the other hand, one expert considers the piece to be a forgery.)

This is an excellent time to contrast classical with neoclassical work, for immediately above the sarcophagus is a statue of the "Three Graces" carved in the nineteenth century by Antonia Canova. One of the original prototypes of this statue is in the Hermitage Palace in Leningrad. The one at the Castle is a copy, probably by a French sculptor named Boyer, about whom nothing else is known. What is more important for the viewer to realize is that nineteenth century sculptors were at one point interested in classical revival. In addition to the "Three Graces," one of Mr. Hearst's favorite statues, other neoclassical works include "Europa and the Bull" by Fritz Behn, "Galatea" in the garden. "Pygmalion and Galatea," by Jean Léon Gérôme, and the statue called "Enchante" by Fredrick William MacMonnies (1863-1927) are in the Main Vestibule. Antonio Canova, the most famous neoclassic sculptor of the nineteenth century, is represented by a statue of Venus in the Assembly Room. Bertol Thorvaldsen, (1770-1844), a Danish sculptor who worked in Italy, is represented by a statue of Venus holding an apple. The apple was given to her by Paris, who judged her to be more beautiful than Juno or Minerva. The four round medallions in the four corners of the Assembly Room are also by Thorvaldsen.

Apulian volute-handled krater — fourth century B.C. (Library).

San Simeon's only example of genuinely Victorian art is this 1890s silver and cloisonne lamp by Tiffany & Co. It is believed to have been the property of Phoebe Apperson Hearst (Assembly Room).

"Madonna and Child and St. John" by Agostino di Duccio, a Florentine sculptor of the late 1400s (North Doge's Bedroom).

The Lower South Duplex contains an exquisite statue of the Greek poet "Anacreon" with a lyre on his back. He is carrying a Bacchanalian putto and a cupid. The authors prefer this statue to all others in the Castle. It is signed by Jean Leon Gerome (1824–1904) and is far superior to the statue in the Main Vestibule by the same artist. Note particularly the handling of the drapery on the bronze Anacreon. Copies of classical statues in marble and bronze are everywhere. The Discus Thrower, or "Discobolos" in bronze, graces the Casa del Sol Terrace below the fountain which is topped by a copy of "David" by Donatello. Discus throwing was one of the original events of the Greek games. The nearly nude statue of David (he does have boots and a hat), portrays David's triumph over Goliath. His foot rests on a shield under which is the head of the giant. Venus (Aphrodite), the goddess of love and beauty, is represented by a number of statues. "Venus of Cyrene" is in the garden near Casa del Monte; "Crouching Venus" is in front of Casa del Monte; and there are several Venuses in the Assembly Room; "Venus Triumphant", "Venus of Canova" and a part of a torso and an authentic Greco Roman antiquity.

Copies of classics also include a bust of Psyche, from the original by Praxiteles, which is in the National Museum in Naples; "Mars and Cupid" by Professor Umberto Marcellini; plus statues of the "Wrestlers", and "Mercury Resting."

The enclosed Roman Pool, while not "Roman," might be

Unidentified portrait by the Dutch painter Godfried Schalken (Casa del Monte).

"The Betrothal of St. Catherine" by an unknown Spanish painter (New Wing).

"Bianca Capello, Duchess of Medici" by Angelo Allori (South Doges Bedroom).

One of a pair of portraits by the Spanish court painter Bartolome Gonzales (Casa del Sol).

considered appropriately nicknamed because of the copies of classical statues. The Romans would have loved the Castle. Highly visible by the door at the West end is a copy of a statue known as the Apoxyomenos by Lysippus. Note the small head in relation to the rest of the body, an example of early deliberate distortion to heighten the effect of the figure. The arms of the statue are extended forward involving the viewer with the action. In the alcove, beneath the newly opened skylight from the tennis court above, is a statue of "Abundantia", a seventeenth century Italian work of great beauty, but located too far from the viewer to be seen in detail.

A large number of ceramic vases from ancient Greece, China, and Persia either stand alone or have had their proportions ruined by the popular practice of wiring them for lamps, a vulgar idea still in practice today. The Greek vase collection has been subjected to closer scrutiny than any other group of objects in the Collection. After Mr. Hearst's death part of the collection was given to the Metropolitan Museum in New York. What remains is still one of the largest private groups. A book should be devoted to this collection alone. Dr. D. A. Amyx, of the University of California, is an authority on Greek vases and has studied the Hearst collection extensively.

When viewing the Greek vases in the Library the visitor will not have enough time to see even a representative sample of all types in the Collection. There are a variety of shapes includ-

At the far end of the Gothic Study hangs a compelling portrait of William Randolph Hearst painted by Orrin Peck in 1894.
Hearst was 31 at the time; the picture is of a quality reminiscent of the portraiture of John Singer Sargent.

Fifteenth-century tempera-on-panel triptych by Giovanni da Piero de Pisa, 1423 (Celestial Sitting Room).

ing amphorae, hydrias, kraters, pithos, rhytons, alabastrans and askos, as well as others. Since most ancient Greek vase painters are unknown, the vases are given names based on the location of their creator's key works, hence the Leningrad painter, etc. There is, in fact, a Hearst painter, so named because his key work exists at Hearst Castle. Most visible to the tourist is the large amphora seen at a distance in the north alcove. This paneled amphora is nicely proportioned and is about thirty-six inches tall. A charming duck askos is visible in the lighted case below the book shelves.

The Persian pitcher found on the nightstand or bed table in Mr. Hearst's bedroom is strikingly contemporary due to the free flowing application of the glaze. The pitcher from Sultanabad, Persia, is from the twelfth century. A number of Majolica ware pieces from Italy exist at the Castle, but none more beautiful than the lamp on the center table in the major top floor room of the New Wing. The visitor can stand close to it and should take advantage of this opportunity. The New Wing also contains a unique Chinese jar from the Marion Davies collection. The jar is now disfigured with a lamp shade.

Look closely and you will see illustrations of smaller jars on the body of the vase.

The strength of the painting collection lies in its emphasis on thirteenth and fourteenth century Italian work and in the personal subject matter of later work. Most memorable is the painting by Orrin Peck of Mr. Hearst as a youth, previously mentioned. It hangs in the center of the Gothic Study, a position whose importance exceeds the quality of the painting.

We illustrate next a relief of Madonna, Child and St. John by Agostino di Duccio which hangs above the fireplace in the North bedroom of the Doge's Suite. Agostino di Duccio was a major figure of the early Renaissance in central Italy. He was responsible for the renovation of the interior of the Church of San Francesco in Rimini, whose exterior was designed by Leon Battista Alberti. This soft polychromed work is beautiful and must be considered a work of major importance in the collection.

The Castle contains numerous primitive Italian works done at a time when most painting went unsigned. One of the most beautiful resides in the Assembly Room where it hangs near

A lamp with a carved crystal Chinese figure as a base and a white silk brocade shade stands in the South Doge's Bedroom.

This sixteenth century presentation case of rock crystal, ebony, and gilt bronze sits atop an Italian Renaissance table in the center of the Assembly Room.

the Canova statue and cannot be seen on the present tour route. The painting is simply called "Madonna and Child with Angels" and is listed as fifteenth century.

The portrait of Bianca Capello, Duchess of Medici, in the South bedroom of the Doge's Suite is by Angelo Allori, a sixteenth-century Florentine painter known as Il Bronzino.

The last painting is one of a pair of portraits. This one is by Bartolome Gonzales, a Spanish court painter of the sixteenth century. It is a portrait of L' infante Clara Isabella Eugenia, sister of Phillip III of Spain and daugher of the famous Phillip II. It hangs in Casa del Sol along with a matching painting of her brother. The historical value of the painting exceeds its value as a work of art. (The furnishings of Casa del Sol are in storage at this writing while damage from the recent bombing is repaired. By the time this book is published the house will have been repaired and the furnishings will again be on display).

Not illustrated in this book, but certainly worth mentioning, are the neoclassical paintings of Jean Leon Gerome in the Celestial Suite, the portrait of Aluisius Vendramin by Jacopo Tintoretto, the major Mannerist painter, along with Veronese of Venice. Two rather stiff portraits of a man and woman by one Ignatio or Juan de Lara are found in Casa del Monte, as well as another pair by Franz Pourbus the Younger, 1597 and 1609. The paintings are for the most part uninspired, but the Annunciation of St. Mary in Casa del Mar by Adriaen Ysenbrandt is beautiful, especially its multicolored angels wings.

The silver items on view at the Castle are probably only a small sample of a much larger collection. Much of the silver is found in the Refectory and is usually well explained on the tour. The Refectory alone contains an Irish mace from Dublin, a silver wine cistern of enormous size from England, candlesticks from France and Spain, a Spanish processional banner in silver, and an assortment of covered dishes from England and Ireland. Their location prevents close study but light from the high windows makes them shine on a bright day. The most visible item of silver is in the Assembly Room. A silver lamp, forty-four inches high, appears to hold the piano in place. Presumably it was previously owned by Phoebe Hearst and was made for her by Tiffany & Co. in New York. The lamp has a silver shade with silver lace.

On the fourth floor of the New Wing is a wood panel covered with repousse silver. The design is an overall pattern of Moorish inspiration and could have been used as a lid for a chest or could have been the left side of a two part door. The room beyond contains an altar tabernacle finished in silver over wood from a church in Spain. The door is decorated with the representation of a pelican, a somewhat uncommon but authentic Christian symbol. The pelican is piercing her breast, so that her chicks can drink her blood and therefore survive in times of limited food supply. The sides of the Tabernacle are decorated with grapes and wheat, symbolizing the sacred bread and wine which was kept inside. The Tabernacle came from the church of San Eil Abord in Spain, made in 1741.

Scattered throughout the Castle are objects carved in jade, rock crystal, or glass. They do not form a cohesive collection but many are choice and, because of their small size, may be easily passed over. A small bedside lamp in the Doge's Suite is made of rock crystal. The visitor passes within a few feet of this object, so it can be examined in detail. Despite the size of the Assembly Room and its welter of art objects, few tourists fail to notice the rock crystal presentation case in the middle of the room. Rene Lalique is a unique figure in decorative artwork in that he worked through both the Art Nouveau period of the 1890s and the Art Deco period of the 1920s and the 1930s. He revolutionized gold jewelry design before 1900, and developed a style of blown glass called lead crystal.

This French artisan is represented by a number of objects at the Castle. The two most likely to be noticed are in the North and South bedrooms of the Doge's Suite. One small bottle in the North bedroom is on the dresser to the left as you enter. The stopper is in the form of a nude girl and the sides of the bottle also have female figures in low-relief. The work is subtle and must be examined with care. The south bedroom has a large vase with four birds standing on the rim.

The few examples we find of this excellent work simply emphasize the fact that had Mr. Hearst been as enthusiastic about contemporary work as he was about massive fireplaces, wood ceilings, and Spanish vargueños, we would now have a much more brilliant collection; but that would have been out of character. The complete absence of Impressionist and Cubist paintings indicates that the Lalique — like the Art Deco lamps, the black plumbing fixtures, the lamp shades, and the Atwater Kent radio — entered the collection either by accident or by necessity. Speculation about what the collection might have been is to miss the point. It remains an enigma as to why a man so interested in contemporary events, in the political and social spheres, should have ignored the brilliant art of his own time.

We have waited until the last to discuss the tapestries because not only are they superior in quality but, taken together, they constitute a wide diversity of styles and techniques. Space limitations in this book prevents a discussion and illustration of each important one, but we can at least alert you to those that appear significant.

The Assembly Room presents us with a wonderful opportunity to enjoy six large tapestries which contrast Mannerist and Baroque styles. The side walls are virtually covered with four great matching hangings designed by Giulio Romano, a sixteenth century artist, in the Mannerist style. They formed part of a larger, ten piece set and were completed around 1550. The set of ten weavings were in the French royal collection prior to the Revolution. We can only assume that the missing six panels have been lost to vandalism. French & Co. sold

Lalique vase with four bird figures on top (South Doge's Bedroom).

Frosted glass bottle with a delicate nymph figuré carved into the stopper is by René Lalique (North Doge's Suite).

To either side of the fireplace stand an exquisite carved chest and an early desk with an elaborately carved center section. They are in Casa del Monte ("B" House).

the four panels to Mr. Hearst in 1921. The scenes represent episodes in the career of Scipio Africanus, Roman general at the time of the Punic Wars. The figures are stiff and crowded together. Giulio Romano was certainly the most talented architect and decorator of the so-called Mannerist period in Italy. Born around 1497, he was still in his teens when he became one of Raphaels' chief assistants in the decoration of the Vatican and the Villa Madama near Rome; departing abruptly for Mantua in northern Italy he developed a practice in that city designing and decorating the principle buildings of the Mannerist period, the Palazzo del Te for the Gonzaga family.

Contrast these tapestries with the circular flowing movement of the Baroque hangings on the end walls. The one at the north end, a single panel, is not to be overlooked. This Peter Paul Rubens design for an allegorical scene depicting the "Triumph of Christianity," as it is usually called, was woven in Brussels in 1625 or thereabout. It is reputed that the original Rubens cartoon for this weaving is in the Prado in Madrid; and it is furthermore assumed (only by some specialists) that the tapestry was part of the dowry of a certain Spanish princess, one Clara Isabella Eugenia, daughter of Philip II of Spain. The point of this anecdote is merely that the tapestry is fine enough and interesting enough that a certain amount of legend has attached itself to the piece over the years. The so-called "Daniel" pair of hangings in the Refectory is medieval in

Another example of a carved chest in the North Doge's Bedroom.

This twenty-five by fourteen foot tapestry is in the Assembly Room and depicts Scipio receiving Carthaginian officers.

French Renaissance cabinet in the sitting room of Casa del Monte.

design with subtle color. They are Gothic in style and may well be the best tapestry set in the Castle. We will pass over the Morning Room tapestries, as they are of no great artistic merit, and go directly to the Billiard Room. The room is dominated by the stunning late Gothic or International Gothic tapestry of a hunting scene with horses, hunting dogs, trees, and flowers. Flowers are strewn on the ground or growing everywhere. This was a typical artistic convention of the late Gothic period. For this reason the tapestry became known as a "thousand flower" variety, although it would be better to refer to it simply as International Gothic. Notice the background figures are not smaller but are placed higher in the composition. At the time this work was being finished, Italian painters like Massacio were already employing a new method of space representation called one point perspective. In terms of content, this hunting scene effectively depicts life in late medieval times. Two more Persian title panels, using the Gothic method of two dimensional space representation, flank the French tapestry.

An ecclesiastical banner hangs above the nuptial bed in the North Bedroom of the Doge's Suite and is of no special interest as to content; but the workmanship and needlework are exquisite and its inclusion here will serve as an example of the numerous ecclesiastical hangings throughout the Castle.

Room One of the fourth floor of the New Wing contains two remarkable tapestries. The main room, whose ceiling has

An ecclesiastical banner hangs above the nuptial bed in the North bedroom of the Doge's Suite.

already been described, has on the west wall a Royal Persian silk rug from Tabriz. The rug has been dated 1782 and is inscribed Ala Akbar, God is great. The hanging is decorated with beautiful calligraphy in Pharsee, an ancient Persian language.

By contrast, the hanging in the bedroom alcove is a rare seventeenth century Spanish tapestry decorated with a coat of arms. The chair at the foot of the bed is Florentine sixteenth century in a double "V" shape.

Most of the rooms in the Castle contain Oriental rugs representing many famous rug making areas of Turkey and Iran. Nearly all are partly covered with tour mats and furniture and are therefore difficult to appreciate. The rugs, tapestries, Greek vases, silver, and ceilings warrant special attention and monographs by specialists in the respective fields. The State of California should be urged to subject the Collection to careful curatorial scrutiny to enhance the benefit the public now receives.

Mr. Hearst is buried in the family tomb at Colma, South of San Francisco. The monument is unmarked to prevent vandalism. His real monument is The Enchanted Hill with its buildings and their contents. It is visited for a variety of reasons by nearly a million people each year. His strengths and weaknesses are on display here for all to see.

Hanging in the New Wing's West Tower is a seventeeth century carpet.

The Castle is dwarfed by the Santa Lucia Mountains to the north.

HOW TO VISIT
THE CASTLE

BY
TAYLOR COFFMAN

Every year during the 1930s, the heyday of Hearst Castle, toward the end of September or the early part of October, William Randolph Hearst moved south from Wyntoon, his summertime Northern California retreat, to his coastal barony at San Simeon. There he stayed, except for an occasional trip to Los Angeles or New York, until sometime in late spring. Hearst, not a man to confine himself to a rigid routine, had nevertheless established a comfortable pattern for his palace-dwelling life in California. His choice of season and locale is not hard to understand. Wyntoon, the Mount Shasta estate, is at its best (not to mention most accessible) in the snow-free summer; whereas, San Simeon enjoys sunshine and balanced temperatures throughout the year. It's not that summers are uninviting or undesirable at San Simeon; indeed, summer, with its burnished clear light, and warm, even tolerably hot days — thanks to semi-arid low humidity — is often a time of magical, almost hypnotic charm on the aptly-named Enchanted Hill. Yet for all his mobility and effort to perfect his pursuit of pleasure, Mr. Hearst could be in but one place at a time. He therefore compromised, as it were, and availed himself of much of the best that his two California Shangrilas could offer.

The traveler of today need suffer from no such dilemma: Wyntoon is still privately owned by the Hearst Corporation; whereas the Castle, State of California-owned since the 1950s, can be visited any time of year (it is closed only on Thanksgiving, Christmas, and New Year's), and each season has its share of advantages and highlights, both for touring the buildings and grounds of La Cuesta Encantada and for traveling through the scenic and historic areas of the surrounding region.

A familiarity with the characteristics — and some of the quirks — of season and climate in this part of California will be of great help in readying not only the out of state traveler, but the Californian as well, for a visit to the Castle. San Simeon — the name, it should be said, refers not only to Hearst's hilltop kingdom but to the greater area surrounding it — is far enough south to be intermittent host to that enviable three-season climate (true winter the only omitted condition) for which Southern California is famous. It is at the same time northerly enough to feel the punch and vigor of Pacific storms equal in intensity to those experienced in many areas of Northern California.

On the Enchanted Hill itself, where the elevation is 1600 feet, 30 to 45 inches of rain from November through April is not uncommon; conversely, a rather unwintry winter yielding only 20 inches of rain with brilliantly clear, seventy-degree days in January and February, followed by the most agreeable of springs, is part of nature's scheme in certain years. Summers can scorch and blaze for weeks on end, with the thermometer reading in the nineties and even topping the hundred-degree mark at times; however, a July or August day during which a heavy, moisture-laden fog causes one to steer clear of dripping palm trees is by no means a freak occurrence. Cloudless days through summer, and through much of the fall, can become so numerous that the appearance of a small puff of white drifting lazily overhead is an event worthy of remark; still other summers find the Mexican-based hurricanes extending their high and balmy fringes, and possibly a brief rain shower, as far north as San Simeon. In short, the Castle is located in a sometimes volatile, sometimes passive transition zone where Pacific Northwest meets Pacific Southwest.

Local weather-watchers delight in these shifts and nuances of season. Alas, the unprepared traveler, lulled by tales of unending sunshine along the golden shore, can be in for a bit of a surprise. It bears saying that no San Simeon-bound traveler should fail to pack an umbrella in his luggage, especially if making a visit during the non-summer months. A stout windbreaker of the ski parka variety or some other kind of weatherproof coat is a must. Off-season travelers who think to pack a raincoat and rubber boots will be more than compensated for their trouble should a mid-winter rainstorm by encountered. And yet swim suits and related gear are not to be left behind regardless of the time of year — windless, mild, exceedingly pleasant weather can settle upon this region, sometimes for a lengthy stay, nearly any time of year, making the beaches around San Simeon a near-tropical delight. It likewise bears mentioning that, in spite of any risks of inclement weather, the rewards of visiting the Castle during the slower, more relaxed weekday periods of the off-season are many.

The Castle is located midway between San Francisco and

La Casa Grande as seen from the South Terrace.

View from the Neptune Terrace of the Neptune Pool.

Los Angeles; the distance from each of the metropolitan areas is some 250 miles and requires a five-hour drive. Access to the San Simeon area, if traced back along the various avenues of approach, can be said to include some of California's finest landscapes. U. S. Highways 1 and 101 run north from Southern California, along some stretches joined together as the same road. At San Luis Obispo the two roads part company; the majority of Castle-bound travelers take Highway 1 to the coast at Morro Bay, renowned for its gigantic rock, and continue north through the verdant seaside town of Cambria to San Simeon.

It is equally scenic to continue along Highway 101 past San Luis Obispo up the imposing Cuesta Grade and over into the upper reaches of the Salinas Valley where, just south of Paso Robles, a new stretch of State Highway 46 crosses the coastal barrier of the Santa Lucias to join Highway 1, a short distance below Cambria and San Simeon. This route offers the traveler a glimpse of pastoral California at its unspoiled best. Upon reaching the summit and beginning the coastward descent, ocean views to the south and west open up panoramically. Many Castle visitors return to points inland by using this segment of Highway 46, espeically if they are northbound and haven't the extra time required for the slower Big Sur portion of Highway 1 north of San Simeon.

Without question, no road to San Simeon rivals the drama, the breathtaking views, the bold magnificence and awesome beauty of the ninety-mile stretch of Highway 1 from San Simeon to Carmel through Big Sur. Indeed, few highways anywhere in the world compare with it. Travelers ply its twisting course both on their way to San Simeon and in leaving the Castle to continue north along the coast. Perhaps the more picturesque approach is the southbound use of this fabled road; upon leaving the curves and hills of the southern end of the Big Sur, one reaches the coastal terrace of the Hearst Ranch and on rounding Piedras Blancas Point the Castle comes into view, jewel-like and seemingly miniature against the blue dome of Pine Mountain. From this angle — seven air miles to the west of the Enchanted Hill and looking eastward — the sheer perfection of the Castle's mountaintop site can be appreciated to the utmost. Interestingly enough, this is a view that few of Hearst's guests were treated to, for the Big Sur highway was not opened until 1937, a relatively late date in the Castle's active history.

The traveler of this route is urged to allow a minimum of three hours of driving time between Carmel and San Simeon. During winter storms, mudslides can close the road for hours or even days; warning signs are conspicuously posted when this happens, and local inquiry is in order to be sure the road is safely negotiable. We would emphasize that gas stations, lodging, and other services are few and far between south of the community of Big Sur itself, roughly two hours of driving time from San Simeon. It is ill-advised for anyone planning a non-stop passage along this ninety-mile stretch to embark from either end of the line with less than two hours of daylight remaining. Not only is the nighttime use of the road potentially hazardous, but the beauty and grandeur of this incomparable region will be missed altogether. In sum, the Big Sur highway is for the traveler who has ample time to savor a matchless sightseeing experience.

Automobile is by far the most common means of journeying to San Simeon. But passenger train, tour bus, and commercial airline provide their share of services to the area as well. Numerous tour buses, for example, escort groups directly to the Visitor Center at the foot of the Enchanted Hill. The Castle is just one of several stops made which, for most bus lines, range from two-day to six-day trips up and down the state. Whether originating in San Francisco and heading south or embarking for points north from Southern California, bus tours normally call at the Danish village of Solvang near Santa Barbara, cruise about the ultra-scenic Carmel-Monterey area, drive along the Big Sur coast, and, without fail, stop at Hearst Castle long enough for their passengers to take a tour. One bus line offers a San Luis Obispo connection when it meets Amtrak's northbound and southbound Coast Starlight, both of which make afternoon stops in San Luis seven days a week. Travelers opting for this tour bus to San Simeon stay overnight in one of the area's motels, tour the Castle the following morning, and then return to San Luis to resume their rail trip in either direction on that afternoon continuation of the Starlight.

A nostalgic morning can be had by taking the Starlight north out of Los Angeles; this is the approach so often used by William Randolph Hearst and his guests years ago. The rural landscape along much of the way is not only unchanged since their time, but is largely no different from what it was in the nineteenth century.

At least one small commercial airline serves San Luis Obispo, thus providing a time-saving connection with California's metropolitan areas. A rental car has to be secured in San Luis by anyone planning to visit the Castle this way. For details of schedules concerning the variations on travel outlined here, consult a travel agency. Travel options will probably be increasing over the coming years, particularly with the cost of gasoline ever on the rise.

San Luis Obispo County's modern age of tourism began with the 1958 opening of the Castle. The year round visitor influx (very heavy during summer and holiday periods and nearing a million visitors a year), has resulted in the proliferation of motels, restaurants, specialty shops, and art galleries throughout the entire county. The community of San Simeon Acres alone — three miles south of the Visitor Center — has 346 rooms among its eight motels; four miles farther south is Cambria, where just under 250 rooms are available. Still farther down Highway 1, yet within comfortable driving distance to the Castle, are Cayucos, Morro Bay, San Luis Obispo, and

Pismo Beach, all offering facilities for those who linger in the area. Local chambers of commerce expend no small amount of effort in keeping brochures and mailing lists up to date. The traveler who wisely decides to plan ahead is encouraged to write for information well in advance (San Simeon Chamber of Commerce, San Simeon, CA 93452; and Cambria Chamber, Cambria, CA 93428). It is of utmost importance that overnight reservations are confirmed for *all* times of year.

Campgrounds in the greater area range from primitive (literally) to developed (toilets and some showers) to those offering mobile-home hookups. Five miles south of the Visitor Center at the Castle is San Simeon State Beach with over 100 developed sites available year round. (Reservations should be made for Memorial Day through Labor Day; other times of year a first come, first served rule applies.) To the north there are two small campgrounds under Federal auspices, Kirk Creek and Plaskett in the middle Big Sur country, and in Big Sur itself the superb Pfeiffer-Big Sur State Park, which offers 184 developed sites (reservations required in summer). South of San Simeon State Beach the nearest campground is at Morro Bay State Park, sylvan in its shoreline setting, followed by the rugged and primeval Montana de Oro State Park, south and across the estuary from Morro Bay. Morro Bay offers 112 developed sites, 18 hookups, and requires reservations at all times of the year; Montana de Oro on the other hand is strictly of the primitive classification. Pismo Beach and environs is a haven for campers of all sorts, whether of the pup tent or Airstream school, where two State Park units, plus facilities provided by privately-owned campgrounds, cater to thousands of vacationers every summer and holiday weekend. The great attraction here is the miles-long white sand beach backed by seemingly endless dunes, ideal for the off-road-vehicle sportsman.

The subject of reservations has been touched on already, but a good deal more may be said about it, for the day to day operation of the Hearst Castle tour program, as well as the booking of sites at State Park campgrounds, have come to depend increasingly on advance scheduling. To put it simply, the days when the traveler could leave Los Angeles in the morning, pull into the Visitor Center sometime in the afternoon, buy a non-reserved ticket for a conveniently scheduled tour, and, upon returning from the Castle, make a leisurely selection of one motel over another for that night's stay, are almost completely a thing of the past. Nowadays not only Californians but people from as far away as the Eastern seaboard take pains to make reservations well in advance of their trip to the Castle. Reserved tickets for tours, as well as for campsites, can be held as much as 60 days prior to the date of use. Actually, as long as reservations are made a few days prior to the desired date, the traveler will be cared for, except perhaps for marathon weekends like Memorial Day and Labor Day.

Travelers from afar who plan to visit other parts of the state before arriving at San Simeon are advised to call the Castle (805-927-4621) or consult your local travel agent in advance. (Or write P.O. Box 8, San Simeon, CA 93452). Tickets can also be bought directly from the ticket office at the Visitor Center, which opens at 8:00 a.m. Ticket prices are naturally subject to change. Let it suffice to say that, at this time, adults are charged one rate; 17-year-olds and younger pay half price; children five or younger can make the tour free of charge provided they sit on an adult's lap while riding the shuttle bus up and down the hill; and school groups are eligible for a discount if taking the tour during the school year and if accompanied by appropriate chaperones. For all tickets bought in advance a nominal reservation charge applies. The only refunds that can be made at the Visitor Center itself are for tickets marked for the same day they are submitted for refund (thus allowing those spaces to be resold on a non-reserved basis that same day). In the event that the traveler is delayed somewhere in the greater area, but thinks he can reach the Castle sometime later in the day than his ticket calls for (it must be the same day), the Visitor Center staff will make every effort to save tour space if notified by phone in advance. Finally, it should be mentioned that tours by wheelchair can now be arranged directly through the Hearst Castle office. Interested parties are asked to make their reservations by phone or mail at least ten days in advance (P. O. Box 8, San Simeon, CA 93452; (805) 927-4621). The wheelchair visitor must provide his own transportation up the hill to the Castle, must be equipped with his own chair, and must be accompanied by someone able to push the wheelchair and its occupant up steep ramps. Cost of the wheelchair tour is the same as the traditional tours.

But what of the tours themselves? First off, it should be made clear that the general public's access to the Castle is strictly on a guided-tour basis. The Hearst Corporation stipulated on donating the Castle to the State of California that commercialization and development of the Enchanted Hill — such as public parking areas, playgrounds for children, and kennels — be kept to an absolute minimum. The State complied by locating its Visitor Center, staging area for the tours, at the foot of the Enchanted Hill, five miles by the driveway of Hearst's time below the Castle itself. And ever since opening day on June 2, 1958, the public has been shuttled up and down the hill by bus.

Until 1964 only one tour route through the Castle, taking in only one fourth of the hilltop layout, was available. This encompassed one of the three smaller buildings (the cottages, or Guest Houses, as they are usually called), highlights of the grounds and gardens, the first floor of La Casa Grande (the main building of the four on the hill) and both swimming pools. With only minor variations on the original route and sequence, this tour is known today as Tour I, the old standby of the present three-tour system. An entire busload of 53 visitors can take Tour I together as a single group: the exterior terraces are

A sight common to Castle visitors, this photograph was taken at some point during the five mile bus ride up to the Castle.

The last giraffe, once a highly prized member of the Hearst Zoo, left San Simeon some forty years ago. The Zoo was disbanded prior to the outbreak of World War II.

spacious enough to accommodate that many people at once, as are the first floor rooms of La Casa Grande, which consume the most time on Tour I. It is an opinion almost universally held by those who know the Castle well that if the visitor has the time for just one tour, it should be Tour I. The larger visitor group it allows might sound like a disadvantage at first; actually, however, the slower movement necessitated by a big group seems to allow the impact and atmosphere of the Enchanted Hill to sink in more deeply, especially if Tour I is the visitor's first exposure to the estate, as it should be. Seeing the most grandiose, and for many San Simeon aficionados, the most memorable of La Casa Grande's numerous rooms — the Theater, the Refectory, the Assembly Room, the Billiard Room — is breathtaking for the visitor.

Tour II, which focuses almost entirely on the upper floors of La Casa Grande, was initiated in 1964 and has proved immensely popular. Its capacity is limited — just a dozen people to a group, due to the relatively restricted spaces through which the tour moves — and thus the need for advance reservations is greater than for either Tour I or Tour III. Undoubtedly what keeps Tour II groups full the year round, seven days a week, is the visitor's anticipation of seeing William Randolph Hearst's private third floor rooms. Indeed, Hearst's Gothic Suite is an architectural and decorative wonder, but the prospective visitor should be aware that the vast majority of rooms in La Casa Grande are guest rooms. Thus Tour II, ideally taken as a follow-up to Tour I, is an overview not only of Hearst's own part of the Castle, but of some of the most fascinating rooms in other parts of the same building. The Doge's Suite, most princely by far of the many guest suites on the hill, is visited; so is the second floor Library, as quietly dignified and magnificent a room as the Castle can boast. (Here the visitor sees a collection of ancient Greek pottery.) The tower-level Celestial Suite and the Kitchen and Pantry are other highlights of Tour II.

As a sequel to the marvels already seen in Tours I and II is Tour III. Like the others, Tour III starts near the outdoor Neptune Pool and then embarks on a course of its own. It first takes in Casa del Monte, smallest of the cottages and host to the much-publicized Cardinal Richelieu Bed. Tour III's route is unique: Casa del Monte represents Hearst's thirty year building program in its first years, the early 1920s; whereas the focus of the tour is on another building, the New Wing of La Casa Grande, where the visitor is shown the results of the final two years of construction at San Simeon (1945–47). It is thus an experience in architectural and decorative contrasts, the earlier San Simeon as against the later. Nearly every room on Tour III is a bedroom, bath, or sitting room for guest use, many of which are connected as three-room suites. The marble-lined bathrooms in the New Wing are, by themselves, nothing short of spectacular. The profusion of Spanish ceilings, lanterns, and doors will be of much interest to those who enjoy vignettes of

Dominating a coastal point of the same name, the Piedras Blancas Lighthouse guards the night seven miles west of the Castle.

A common view of the coastline along Big Sur Highway from one of many bridges built in the 1930s during the Works Progress Administration.

a bygone 1920s California splendor. But, amazingly enough, as though there were some kind of time-warp, there is much of the late 1940s in the New Wing as well.

Visitors who take all three tours will come satisfactorily close to seeing as much of the Enchanted Hill as it is possible to see. It should be remembered though that each tour requires its own bus ride up and down the hill, there is no option of remaining on the hill after completing one tour while waiting for another. (The State has experimented in the past with combination, stay-on-the-hill multiple tours but they simply did not work out.) Each tour, including travel time, lasts one hour and forty-five minutes, of which one hour and fifteen minutes is spent being conducted about the Castle grounds and through the buildings. A back-to-back trek on Tours I, II, and III, complete with three round-trip, ten-mile bus rides — a round robin made by no small number of visitors every year — takes just under six hours . . . provided the visitor has obtained tickets marked at exact two-hour intervals.

Considering the number of stairs involved — 150 on Tour I and some 300 each for Tours II and III — the more leisurely visitor with time at his disposal will very likely prefer a longer break between tours than the mere ten or fifteen minutes allowed by the straight-through approach. An ideal pace and sequence, it would seem, would be to take Tour I in the morning, when the charm of the place comes across fully in a lower angle of light, followed by an afternoon trip on Tour II. The next morning could be spent taking Tour III, the visitor having had adequate time in the interim to reflect on all that had been seen the previous day. An alternate suggestion is to take Tour I in the afternoon followed by Tour II the next morning, and if the visitor is interested in still more, Tour III after that. Unfortunately, the great need for advance reservations works against the visitor's deciding on the spur of the moment to take a third tour; if one has even a vague feeling that nothing short of all three tours is what he wants, he should go ahead and make plans accordingly. Chances are he'll be wishing he could see still more after the three tours are over.

Those who desire longer breaks between tours will find much to do in the general area, especially if the lag time is several hours. A walk on nearby beaches, well supplied with driftwood and other interesting ocean debris, might result in the spotting of a California gray whale just outside the thick kelp beds or, even closer to shore, the sleek sea otter of these coastal waters. Across the highway from the Visitor Center is the very Spanish-looking village of San Simeon, largely a Hearst creation, complete with a warehouse that will fool nearly anyone into mistaking it for an old California mission. A vintage building in San Simeon is the pre-Hearst Sebastian's Store of 1852. Its collection of memorabilia from nineteenth-century San Simeon, the whaling port, is worth a peek inside. For those content merely to loll about the Visitor Center while awaiting a tour, a few picnic tables and a snack bar and souvenir shop are at hand.

Other visitors to the area will want to take a short drive up the coast to the lower end of Big Sur county, especially if their plans call for a departure from the San Simeon area in the opposite direction. South of the Castle, the communities of San Simeon Acres and Cambria are close enough to allow for between-tour gallery-browsing and such. Still more time will allow for a trip to the other side of the coastal summit open throughout the year. In all, the visitor will find much besides the Castle itself — though it unquestionably has no rival among attractions in the area — to persuade him to stay longer in the region or at least to return to this lovely and uncommon part of California someday.

CHRONOLOGY

1821: George Hearst is born near Sullivan, Franklin County, Missouri (September 3).

1842: Phoebe Apperson is born (December 3).

1850: George Hearst departs for California.

1860: George Hearst returns to Missouri upon hearing the news of his mother's illness.

1862: George Hearst and Phoebe Apperson elope and are married (June 15).

1863: George and Phoebe Hearst arrive in San Francisco, California. William Randolph Hearst is born in San Francisco (April 29).

1872: Julia Morgan is born in San Francisco (January 26).

1874: William Randolph Hearst and Phoebe Hearst depart on their first trip to Europe.

1876—1881: William Randolph Hearst attends St. Paul's School, Concord, New Hampshire.

1880: Second trip to Europe for William Randolph Hearst with his mother, Phoebe Hearst.

1881: Millicent Willson is born.

1882: William Randolph Hearst enrolls in Harvard University.

1885: William Randolph Hearst leaves Harvard, goes to Washington, D.C., and takes a house with his mother, Phoebe.

1886: George Hearst is appointed to the United States Senate, Senator from California (March 23).

1887: George Hearst is elected, by the California Legislature, to the United States Senate (January).
William Randolph Hearst takes over the *Examiner* newspaper (March).

1890: Julia Morgan enrolls at the University of California, Berkeley.

1891: George Hearst dies in Washington, D.C., (March 1).

1894: Julia Morgan graduates with a B.S. in Civil Engineering and decides to continue her studies in Paris.

1896: Phoebe Apperson Hearst sponsors an international architectural competition for plans for the grounds and buildings of the University of California campus, Berkeley.

1897: William Randolph Hearst meets Millicent Willson.
Phoebe Hearst is appointed Regent of the University of California.

1898: Julia Morgan finally, after much work, gains admission to L'Ecole des Beaux-Arts (November 9).

1900: Marion Davies is born in New York (January 3).

1901—1902: Julia Morgan complets her studies at L'Ecole and returns to Oakland. She goes to work drafting for John Galen Howard, the winner of Phoebe's international competition for designing the U.C. campus at Berkeley.

1902: William Randolph Hearst meets Julia Morgan at the "Hacienda" in Pleasanton.
William Randolph Hearst is elected to the United States Congress from the 11th District of New York and serves from 1903–1907.
Construction begins on the Hearst Memorial Mining Building on the University of California campus, Berkeley.

1903: William Randolph Hearst and Millicent Willson marry (April 28).

1904: George Randolph Hearst is born, first son of William and Millicent Hearst.

1905: William Hearst is an unsuccessful candidate for New York mayor, on the Municipal ticket.

1908: William Randolph Hearst, Jr. is born, second son of William and Millicent Hearst (January 27).
Completion of the Hearst Memorial Mining Building ($645,000).

1909: John Randolph Hearst is born, third son of William and Millicent Hearst.
William Randolph Hearst is unsuccessful candidate for New York mayor, on the Independent League ticket.

1915: Randolph Apperson and Albert Willson (David Whitmere, twin-sons of William and Millicent Hearst born (December 3).

1918: William Randolph Hearst meets Marion Davies.

1919: Phoebe Hearst dies at the "Hacienda" in Pleasanton, California (April 13).
William Randolph Hearst decides to build at San Simeon. He visits Julia Morgan in San Francisco, and the work is under way.
Construction starts on the Enchanted Hill.

1920: La Casa del Mar (The House of the Sea), first of the buildings on the hilltop, is completed.

1921: La Casa del Monte (The House of the Mountains) is completed.

1922: La Casa del Sol (The House of the Sun) is completed.

1921—1947: La Casa Grande (The Large House) is under construction.

1926: La Casa Grande is occupied by William Randolph Hearst for the first time (December).

1947: William Randolph Hearst leaves San Simeon and the Enchanted Hill for the last time and goes to live with Marion Davies in Beverly Hills.

1951: William Randolph Hearst dies and is buried in Cypress Lawn Cemetery, Colma, California (August 14).

1957: Julia Morgan dies (February).

1961: Marion Davies dies (September).

197?: Millicent Hearst dies.

GLOSSARY

alabaster 1. a compact, fine-textured, usually white and translucent gypsum often carved into vases and ornaments. 2. a hard, compact calcite or aragonite that is translucent and sometimes banded.

altar frontal altar facing, as seen from the front.

altarpiece a work of art that decorates the space above and behind an altar.

amphora 1. an ancient Greek jar or vase with a large oval body, narrow cylindrical neck, and two handles that rise almost to the level of the mouth. 2. a two-handled vessel shaped like an amphora.

anvil a heavy, usually steel-faced iron block on which metal is shaped (as by hand hammering).

arch a typically curved structure member spanning an opening and serving as a support (as for the wall or other weight above the opening).

armillary sphere an old astronomical instrument composed of rings representing the positions of the orbits of important celestial bodies.

armorial of, relating to, or bearing heraldic arms.

Art Deco a pervasive, decorative style of the 1920s and 1930s characterized especially by bold outlines, streamlined and rectilinear forms, and the use of new materials such as plastics.

art glass articles of glass designed primarily for decorative purposes, especially novelty glassware.

artifact 1. a usually simple object, (as a tool or ornament) showing human workmanship or modification. 2. a product of civilization. 3. a product of artistic endeavor.

Art Nouveau a decorative style of late 19th century origin characterized especially by sinuous lines and foliated forms.

associationalism of or pertaining to an association, union or confederation.

aureole a quadrangular, circular, or elliptic halo or frame surrounding the figure of Christ, the Virgin, or certain saints.

balustrades a row of balusters topped by a railing, also a low parapet or barrier.

banner a piece of cloth attached by one edge to a staff and used by a monarch, feudal lord, or commander as his standard and as a rallying point in battle.

baroque of, relating to, or having the characteristics of a style of artistic expression prevalent especially in the 17th century, marked generally by extravagant forms and elaborate and sometimes grotesque ornamentation: characterized specifically in architecture by dynamic opposition and the use of curved and plastic figures; in music by improvisation, contrasting effects, and powerful tensions; and in literature by complexity of form and bizarre, ingenious, and often ambiguous imagery.

bas-relief sculptural relief in which the projection from the surrounding surface is slight, and no part of the modeled form is undercut.

benitier a holy water stoup or vessel for liquids.

brazier a pan for holding burning coals.

bust a sculptured representation of the upper part of the human figure, including the head and neck and usually part of the shoulders and breast.

Celestial Sitting Room fireguard crafted from brass and iron by an unknown artisan during the 1920s.

capital   the crowning feature of a column or pilaster.

Carillon bells   a set of fixed chromatically tuned bells, sounded by hammers controlled from a keyboard.

caryatid   a draped female figure supporting an entablature; a sculptured female figure used as a column or support.

cassone   a large Italian chest with hinged lid, often decorated with carving or painting.

cassowary   any of several large ratite birds of New Guinea, Australia, and the Aru Islands, closely related to the emu, with a horny casque on the head, swift runners, inhabiting woods and jungles.

castle   a large fortified building or set of buildings. Anything resembling or likened to a castle; as any massive, strong, or imposing house or mansion.

cast stone   concrete cast to resemble stone.

celestial   1. of, relating to, or suggesting heaven or divinity. 2. of or relating to the sky or visible heavens.

chasuble   a sleeveless outer vestment worn by the officiating priest at mass.

choir stalls   a seat in the choir of a church, enclosed wholly or partly at the back and sides, often canopied and elaborately carved.

cista   a box or chest, especially for sacred utensils.

classic   of or relating to the first class or rank. In accordance with a coherent system of authoritative principles, in art, literature, architecture, etc.

cloister   a covered passage on the side of a court, usually having one side walled and the other an open arcade or colonnade.

colonnade   a range of columns.

column   a supporting pillar.

concrete   a hard, strong building material made by mixing a cementing material (a portland cement) and a mineral aggregate (as sand and gravel) mass.

contextual   of, pertaining to, or conforming to the context.

cope   a long enveloping ecclesiastical vestment.

cornice   in Classic or Renaissance architecture, the crowning or upper portion of the entablature; any crowning projection.

credenza   a sideboard, buffet, or bookcase patterned after a Renaissance credence; especially one without legs.

diptych   1. a two-leaved, hinged tablet, folding together to protect writing on its waxed surfaces. 2. a picture or series of pictures (as an altarpiece) painted or carved on two hinged tablets.

diorite   a granular, crystaline, igneous rock consisting of acid, plagioclase, and hornblende.

doge   the chief magistrate in the republics of Venice and Genoa.

eclectic   selecting or choosing, as doctrines or methods, from various sources, systems, etc.

egg and dart   an egg shaped ornament, alternating with another in the form of a dart, or anchor, or tongue; also called egg and anchor or tongue.

enamelled   1. to cover, inlay, or decorate with enamel. 2. to beautify with a color surface.

entablature   the upper section of a wall or story usually supported on columns or pilasters and consisting of architrave, frieze and cornice; also any similar part, as an elevated support for a machine part.

espaliered   a plant, as a fruit tree, trained to grow flat against a support such as a wall or trellis.

esplanade   a level open stretch of paved or grassy ground.

facade   the front of a building; any other face, as on a street or court, of a building given special architectural treatment.

faldistorium or faldistory   the seat of a bishop within a chancel.

faldstool   1. a folding stool or chair; specifically one used by a bishop. 2. a folding stool or small desk at which one kneels during devotions; especially on used by the sovereign of England at his coronation. 3. the desk from which the litany is read in Anglican churches.

frieze   an ornamented band; that part of an entablature between the architrave and the cornice, sometimes enriched with sculpture.

fireguard   fire screen; protected and often ornamented screen before a fireplace.

gable   the triangular portion of a wall, between the enclosing lines of a sloping roof.

gothic   1. of, relating to, or resembling the Goths, their civilization, or their language. 2. of, relating to, or having the characteristics of a style of architecture developed in northern France and spreading through western Europe from the middle of the 12th century to the early 16th century, characterized by the converging of weights and strains at isolated points upon slender vertical piers and counterbalancing buttresses, and by pointed arches and vaulting.

hanaper   a receptacle for plate or treasure; a treasure box; a kind of small hamper in which documents were kept.

herm   a statue in the form of a square stone pillar surmounted by a bust or head, especially of Hermes.

high-relief   sculptural relief in which at least half of the circumference of the modeled form projects.

lectern   a desk or stand from which scripture lessons are read in a church service.

limestone   a rock consisting chiefly of calcium carbonate, usually an accumulation of organic remains such as shells, which yields lime when burned.

linenfold carvings   a type of relief ornament, imitating folded linen, carved on the face of individual timber panels. Popular in the late 15th and 16th century.

lintel   a horizontal timber or stone, also known as the architrave, that spans an opening.

loggia   a roofed open gallery, especially at an upper story overlooking an open court.

mace   1. a heavy, often spiked staff or club used especially in the Middle Ages for breaking armor. 2. an ornamental staff borne as a symbol of authority before a public official or legislative body.

mannerist/mannerism   a term of recent invention coined to describe the characteristics of the output of Italian Renaissance architects of the period 1530–1600.

mantel   1. a beam, stone, or arch serving as a lintel to support the masonry above a fireplace; the finish around a fireplace. 2. a shelf above a fireplace.

marriage chest   a bridal chest, used for the accumulation of a trousseau.

mazer   a large drinking bowl originally of hardwood.

medallion   1. a large medal. 2. something resembling a large medal; especially a tablet or panel in a wall or

Of the two window grilles depicted, one is from seventeenth century Spain. The other is a copy from the 1920s. Like so many other things at the Castle, the reproduction is so skillfully crafted it is indistinguishable from the original.

window bearing a figure in relief, a portrait, or an ornament.

misericord or **misericorde**   a thin-bladed, medieval dagger for giving the death or "mercy" stroke.

mosaic   a surface decoration made by inlaying small pieces of variously colored material to form pictures or patterns.

neo-classic   belonging to or designating a revival of classical taste and style in art, literature, architecture, etc.

niche   a recess in a wall, a hollowed space in a wall, made especially for a statue, bust, or other ornament.

pediment   a triangular space forming the gable of a two-pitched roof in classical architecture.

pergola   1. arbor, trellis. 2. a structure usually consisting of parallel colonnades supporting an open roof of girders and cross rafters.

pewter   any of various alloys having tin as chief component, especially a dull alloy with lead, formerly used for domestic utensils.

pilaster   an upright architectural member, rectangular in plan and structurally a pier, but architecturally treated as a column, usually projecting a third of its width or less from the wall.

pithos   a large, casklike vessel of earthenware, frequently made without a base since such jars were often set in the earth; found throughout the Greek world.

plaque   a flat, thin piece of metal, ivory or the like used, as on a wall, for ornamentation, inserted in furniture, etc.

polychrome   relating to, made with, or decorated in several colors.

pricket   1. a spike on which a candle is stuck. 2. a candlestick with such a point.

prie-dieu   1. a kneeling bench designed for use by a person at prayer and fitted with a raised shelf on which the elbows or a book may be rested. 2. a low, armless, upholstered chair with a high, straight back.

refectory   a dining hall, especially in a monastery.

Reja screen   an ornate, iron grille or screen; a characteristic feature of Spanish church interiors.

reliefs   in sculpture, the projection of figures, ornaments, etc. from a background; a work of art so produced. The kinds of relief are named according to the degree of projection.

reliquary   a container or shrine in which sacred relics are kept.

renaissance   the term applied to the reintroduction of classical architecture all over Europe in the 15th and 16th centuries.

repoussé   1. shaped or ornamented with patterns in relief made by hammering or pressing on the reverse side, especially of metal. 2. formed in relief.

salt-cellar   a small vessel for holding salt at the table.

sarcophagus   a stone coffin usually richly carved.

sconce   a bracket candlestick or group of candlesticks; an electric fixture patterned on a candle sconce.

soffit   the ceiling or underside of any architectural member.

spandrel   1. the sometimes ornamented space between the right or left exterior curve of an arch and an enclosing right angle. 2. the triangular space beneath the string of a stair.

statue   a three-dimensional representation usually of a person, animal, or mythical being, reproduced by sculpturing, modeling, or casting.

statuette   a small statue.

tabernacle   a receptacle for the consecrated elements of the Eucharist, especially an ornamental locked box fixed to the middle of the altar and used for reserving the host.

tapestry   a heavy, handwoven, reversible textile used for hangings, curtains, and upholstery and characterized by complicated pictorial designs.

tazza   a shallow cup or vase on a pedestal.

tempera   a process of painting in which an albuminous or colloidal medium (as egg yolks) is employed as a vehicle instead of oil.

terrace   1. a colonnaded porch or promenade; a flat roof or open platform; a relatively level paved or planted area adjoining a building. 2. a raised embankment with the top leveled.

terra cotta   1. a glazed or unglazed fired clay used especially for statuettes, vases, and architectural purposes as roofing, facing and relief ornamentation.

torchière/torchère   a small, high, delicate candlestand used in the 18th century, usually having a tripod base.

travertine   a mineral consisting of a massive, usually layered calcium carbonate (as aragonite or calcite) formed by deposition from spring waters, especially from hot springs.

triptych   1. an ancient Roman writing tablet with three waxed leaves hinged together. 2. a set of three panels or compartments side by side, bearing pictures, carvings, or the like.

truncated pyramid   the part of a pyramid left when its vertex is cut off by a plane usually parallel to its base.

tympanum   a recessed face of a pediment within the frame made by the upper and lower cornices, usually a triangular space or table. The space within an arch, and above a lintel or a subordinate arch, spanning the opening below the arch.

vargueno   a decorative cabinet of a form originating in Spain, the body being rectangular, and supported on legs or on ornamental framework and the front opening downwards on hinges to serve as a writing desk.

verd-antique   a green, mottled or veined serpentine marble, or calcareous serpentine, much used for indoor decorations, especially by the ancient Romans.

vestibule   an ante-room to a larger apartment of a building.

vestment   a garment; especially a garment or robe of ceremony or office; also clothing; garb; dress. A liturgical garment; any article of ceremonial attire and insignia worn by officiants and assistants during divine service, as appropriate to the rite and indicative of their hierarchical rank.

villa   1. a country estate. 2. the rural or suburban residence of a wealthy person.

votive panel   given by vow, or in fulfillment of a vow or promise, or in devotion; consecrated by a vow.

wellhead   a source of a spring, or a stream fountainhead; the top of a structure built over a well.

BIBLIOGRAPHY

Aina, Rose Hollenbaugh *Spanish and Mexican Land Grants in California*. Thesis at the University of California, Berkeley, 1932. Reprinted in 1973 by R. & E. Associates, Saratoga, California.

Alexander, J. "Cellini to Hearst to Klotz." *Saturday Evening Post,* November 1, 1941.

Bean, Walton *California: An Interpretive History.* New York: McGraw-Hill, 1973.

Bemelmans, Ludwig *Fortieth One I Love the Best.* New York: Viking Press, 1955.

Bernhardi, Robert *The Buildings of Berkeley.* Oakland, California: The Holmes Book Co., 1972.

Bliven, B. "Hearst the Hell Raiser." *New Republic,* August 27, 1951.

Bonfils, Winifred *The Life and Personality of Phoebe Apperson Hearst.* San Francisco: J. H. Nash, 1928.
A very complimentary biography of Phoebe Hearst.

Boulian, Dorothy *Enchanted Gardens of Hearst Castle.* Cambria, California: Phildor Press, 1972.

Carlson, Oliver *Brisbane.* New York: Stackpole Sons, 1937.

Carlson, Oliver *Hearst, Lord of San Simeon.* New York: Viking Press, 1936.
As the title suggests, not a flattering portrayal.

Chase, Ilka *Past Imperfect.* Garden City, New York: Doubleday, Doran & Co., 1942.

Clemons, C. "William Randolph Hearst: Great Collector." *Hobbies,* October, 1951.

Cobb, Irving S. *Exit Laughing.* New York: Bobbs-Merrill, 1941.

Coblentz, D. and McDonald, D. "He pulled all the strings." *Commonweal,* August 1, 1952.

Coblentz, Edmond D. *W. R. Hearst: A Portrait in His Own Words.* New York: Simon and Schuster, 1952.
Probably closest to an autobiography.

Crane, F. "My Visit to San Simeon." *New Yorker,* April 5, 1941.

Crowther, Bosley *Hollywood Raja.* New York: n.p., 1960.

Davies, Marion *The Times We Had.* Indianapolis: Bobbs-Merrill, 1975.
Marion's life with W. R. Hearst "as she remembered it."

Didion, Joan "Trip to Xanadu; San Simeon Estate." *Saturday Evening Post,* September 21, 1968.

Failing, P. "William Randolph Hearst's Enchanted Hill." *Art News,* January, 1979.

Giles, Fred Lawrence *Marion Davies.* n.p., n.d.
Marion's biography—More or less.

Hamilton, Geneva *Where the Highway Ends: Cambria, California:* Williams Printing, 1974.
History of Cambria and San Luis Obispo County.

Hearst, George *The Way It Was.* n.p. Hearst Corporation, 1972.
Autobiographical writings of George Hearst.

Hearst, J. R., Jr. "Life with Grandfather." *Reader's Digest,* May, 1960.

Hearst, William Randolph *Selections from the Writings and Speeches of William Randolph Hearst.* San Francisco: Published privately, 1948.

Heizer, Robert F. *Handbook of North American Indians. Volume 8: California.* Washington, D.C.: Smithsonian Institution, 1978.

Hillmen, G. T. "Onward and Upward with the Arts: Monastery for Sale." *New Yorker,* February 1, 1941.

Iona, S. "Pleasures and Palaces." *Saturday Evening Post,* July, 1978.

Kael, P. "Onward and Upward with the Arts." *New Yorker,* February 20, 1971.

Kelley, Florence Finch *Flowing Stream.* New York: E.P. Dutton, n.d.

Kraft, V. "Meanwhile Back at the Hearst Ranch." *Sports Illustrated,* December 13, 1976.

Lewis, Oscar *Fabulous San Simeon.* San Francisco: California Historical Society, 1958.

Libling, A. J. "Wayward Press." *New Yorker,* September 8, 1951.

Longstreth, Richard W. *Julia Morgan, Architect.* Berkeley, California: Berkeley Architectural Heritage Association, 1977.

Lundberg, Ferdinand *Imperial Hearst.* New York: Equinox Cooperative Press, 1936.
A biography slanted against W. R. Hearst.

Moley, Raymond "Hearst Traditions." *Newsweek,* August 27, 1951.

Mott, F. L. "Treacherous Titan." *Saturday Evening Review,* November 1, 1952.

Murray, Ken *The Golden Days of San Simeon.* Garden City, New York: Doubleday, 1971.
Just look at the pictures.

Newton, A. E. "Tourist in Spite of Himself: At the Hearst Ranch." *Atlas,* October, 1932.

O'Laughlin, Edward T. *Hearst and His Enemies.* New York: Arno, 1970.
Newspaper accounts of Hearst's activities.

Older, Cora M. B. *William Randolph Hearst, American.* New York: Appleton, 1936.
Biography which makes Hearst a saint.

Older, Fremont *The Life of George Hearst.* Los Angeles: Westernlore, 1966.
Very complimentary biography of George Hearst.

Older, Fremont *George Hearst, California Pioneer.* Los Angeles: Westernlore, 1966.

Rathbone, O. "Happy Birthday, William Randolph Hearst." *Esquire,* December 1972.

Richey, Elinor *Eminent Women of the West.* Berkeley, California: Howell-North Books, 1975.
Read chapter on Julia Morgan.

St. Johns, Adela Rogers *The Honeycomb.* New York: New American Library, 1970.
Good newspaper and W. R. Hearst background.

Santayana, George *Persons and Places.* New York: Charles Scribner's Sons, 1944.

Seldes, George *Lords of the Press.* New York: J. Messner Inc., 1938.
Labor's case against Hearst.

Steffens, Lincoln "Hearst, Man of Mystery." *The American Magazine,* November, 1906.

Swanberg, W. A. *Citizen Hearst, a Biography of William Randolph Hearst.* New York: Charles Scribner & Sons, 1961.

Swing, Raymond Gram *Forerunners of American Capitalism.* New York: Julian Messner, 1935.

Taloumis, G. "Hearst Gardens." *Horticulture,* December, 1968.

Taylor, F. J. "Incredible House that Hearst Built." *Saturday Evening Post,* May 9, 1959.

Tebbel, John William *The Life and Good Times of William Randolph Hearst.* New York: Dutton, 1952.
A good biography.

Torre, Susana. *Women in American Architecture: A Historic and Contemporary Perspective.* New York: Watson-Guptill Publications, 1977.

Towner, Wesley *Elegant Auctioneers.* New York: Hill & Wang, 1970.
The millionaire collectors . . . an absolute must!

Upton, Dexter C. *The Piping and Purification System of the Hearst State Historical Monument.* Unpublished senior project, San Luis Obispo, California: California Polytechnic University, 1972.

Veiller, Bayard *The Fun I've Had.* New York: Reynal, 1941.
Background on W. R. Hearst as a movie producer.

Winkler, John K. *W. R. Hearst, An American Phenomenon.* New York: Simon and Schuster, 1928.

ANONYMOUS BIBLIOGRAPHY

"Bobby-Trapped" *Time,* March 15, 1948.

"California Here I Go—Hearst" *Literary Digest,* August 26, 1936.

"Death Enters the Barred Portals" *Christian Century,* August 29, 1951.

"Fifteen Million Worth: Collection of Art and Art Objects" *Time,* March 14, 1938.

"Fifty Years of Hearst" *Time,* March 15, 1937.

"First Citizen Hearst" *Golden West,* July, 1974.

"Hail and Farewell" *Time,* August 27, 1951.

"Head Men in the Hearst Empire" *Time,* August 27, 1951.

"Hearst Art on the Counter" *Newsweek, January 16, 1941.*

"Hearst at Eighty-Five" *Newsweek,* May 10, 1948.

"Hearst Carries On" *Nation,* March 7, 1942.

"Hearst Castle in San Simeon—Other Ways to Get There" *Sunset,* April, 1976.

"Hearst Empire" *Business Week,* September 22, 1931.

"Hearst Housecleaning" *Newsweek,* October 8, 1951.

"Hearst is Eighty" *Time,* May 10, 1943.

"Hearst Journalism" *Life,* August 27, 1951.

"Hearst Redivivus" *Time,* February 5, 1945.

"Hearst Self-Portrait" *Newsweek,* July 23, 1952.

"Hearst Treasures on the Block" *Arts and Decoration,* January, 1939.

"Hearst's Bombshell" *Time,* September 3, 1951.

"Hearst's Fabulous Art Goes At Bargain Prices" *Life,* February 10, 1941.

"Hedda Cuts a Queen" *Newsweek,* September 3, 1951.

"House That Hearst Built" *Newsweek,* August 29, 1966.

"Jigsaw Puzzle: Monastery from Sacramenia" *Time,* January 11, 1954.

"King is Dead" *Time,* August 20, 1951.

"Major Liquidation: Hearst's Art Treasures" *Time,* January 6, 1941.

"Marion Davies, Consultant" *Time,* November 5, 1951.

"May 17 Hearsts' Fantastic San Simeon Opens to the Public" *Sunset,* May, 1958.

"Mr. Hearst Can't Take It" *New Republic,* January 20, 1941.

"New Ways for Hearstdom" *Business Week,* November 3, 1951.

"News for the Chief" *Time,* May 28, 1949.

"Number Two Man" *Time,* May 7, 1945.

"Obituary: George Hearst" *Harpers Weekly,* March 14, 1891.

"Passing of the Crown" *Newsweek,* August 27, 1951.

"Past Tradition: Choice Items from the Collection of William Randolph Hearst" *Country Life,* July, 1939.

"Quiet Revolution" *Time,* May 26, 1952.

"San Simeon Revisited" *Time,* November 18, 1966.

"Seer of San Simeon" *Newsweek,* May 6, 1946.

"Shaking the Empire" *Time,* December 31, 1951.

"Sixty Years of Hearst" *Time,* March 17, 1947.

"Spanish Song" *Time,* December 16, 1940.

"To San Simeon's Taste" *Newsweek,* February 4, 1946.

"Unique Tour of San Simeon" *Life,* August 26, 1957.

"William Randolph Hearst" *Life,* August 27, 1951.

"William Randolph Hearst" *Nation,* August 25, 1951.

"William Randolph Hearst Empire: Publisher Decides to Give Up His $15,000,000 Art" *Newsweek,* March 14, 1938.

LIST OF ILLUSTRATIONS

Note: Page references are italicized.

PHOTO CREDITS

INDEX

Numerals in italics indicate illustrations